SCIENTIFIC SAILBOAT RACING

SCIENTIFIC SAILBOAT RACING

BY TED WELLS

With Photographs and Drawings

REVISED AND ENLARGED EDITION

DODD, MEAD & COMPANY · **NEW YORK**

Introduction

The best thing about racing sailboats as a hobby is that no one is ever so good that he cannot be beaten, and no one is ever so poor that he doesn't have a chance.

The sentence above started the introduction to the first edition of *Scientific Sailboat Racing*. Since this first edition was published in 1950, naturally many things have changed—hence this new revised and enlarged edition. That sentence however still sums up my opinion on sailboat racing as a hobby —I'm only going to enlarge on it a bit.

Identical conditions never occur twice—there is always at least a little variation—so there is no chance of getting bored with sailing races. Almost every situation will, however, be followed sometime later—maybe once a month, maybe once a season, or maybe only once every several years—by a new situation just close enough to the previous one so that if you are wide awake, you can profit by what you learned the first time a similar situation occurred. No chance for boredom but a chance to profit by experience.

This book really pertains only to racing of small sailboats. I know nothing about racing big boats—but from the limited experience I have had with them, I would say that some big boat skippers would do a lot better if they had some small boat racing experience. I don't care how big the boat is —you still have to sail it properly to win races. The alibis are a lot easier to come by on a big boat that is out of sight of the others most of the time. When the skipper goofs in a small boat race, the fact, and generally the reason, are both immediately obvious—not only to the skipper, but to a lot of other people. You learn faster when you don't have a chance to use alibis.

When I first started winning races with some consistency some years ago, everyone assumed that it was my experience with airplanes and my supposedly superior knowledge of aerodynamics that was my secret for success. I finally got tired of explaining that a knowledge of theoretical aerodynamics was a hindrance, if anything, and that there wasn't any Arthur-Murray-In-a-Hurry method of learning how to win races, so I wrote the first edition of this book.

I still feel that a technical knowledge of airplanes, or of any other branch of science for that matter, is of no value in learning how to win sailing races, but a scientific and analytical approach to solving the problems of winning races is of the greatest importance. The danger with the scientific approach seems to be that with some people this approach tends to go blindly down one of two alleys—preoccupation with either sails or hull lines, ignoring the people who are in the boat.

Three factors are important in winning races: The boat must be good, the sails must be good, and the skipper-and-crew combination must be good. All are important. It is impossible to say definitely which is the most important—except that there are still too many skippers who don't look in the mirror when they are looking for reasons for not winning races.

A good skipper can trade boats and sails with an inexperienced skipper in a race, and if the boats and sails are not too unequal, the good skipper will beat the inexperienced one in the race by about as big a margin as he would have without trading. Of course, if you are going to take your racing seriously there is no point in handicapping yourself by not having a boat and sails that are as good as the best.

In one-design classes, all boats can be, but frequently aren't, as good as the best. There is no reason, however, why an old boat that is not in completely hopeless condition cannot be made to equal the best, and with a new boat there just should be no reason at all for alibis. Sails, if they have been made by a sailmaker who has a reputation for making good sails for the class you are sailing in, are awfully close to identical. An occasional lemon may show up, but in most cases, the problem is knowing how to use them to the best advantage. Developing a good skipper-and-crew combination is by far the most difficult problem. It requires learning how to get the most out of the boat and sails under all conditions, making the correct tactical decisions almost without thinking, and doing a minimum of dumb things.

It is a good idea to keep notes on your races, listing the sails used, the wind and water conditions, any particularly bright or dumb things done, and what happened and why. Studying these notes frequently will be very valuable—either for the beginner or for the expert. Reviewing this book now and then won't hurt either. It is amazing how things which just slide by the first few times finally ring a bell in the light of later experience.

What scientific sailboat racing really amounts to is to base your conclusions only on facts which have been carefully observed, analyzed, and classified—then to make the most of them.

Contents

CONTENTS

PART IV. SOME RANDOM REFLECTIONS FROM EXPERIENCE

Illustrations

ILLUSTRATIONS

PART I

Making Your Boat and Sails Equal to the Best

I. Tuning the Boat

A POPULAR EXCUSE FOR NOT WINNING RACES IS, "MY BOAT WASN'T TUNED up properly." This implies that there is some deep, dark mystery involved and that if the skipper could only find something on the boat that he could pull, shove, or twist a microscopic amount he would start winning races. This is a lot of baloney. A boat which is in hopelessly bad shape and has never won any races cannot be made good enough to win races with a little twiddling here and there. On the other hand, if a boat has consistently placed well and suddenly starts placing poorly, the chances are pretty good that it isn't the boat that needs tuning up—it is the skipper.

In most one-design classes there is not enough difference between the maximum and minimum permissible dimensions so that there can possibly be any significant difference between boats as a result of differences in hull lines. Many skippers, even those with long experience, will not agree with this statement. As an example, they will point to the fact that a certain skipper who never got near the top bought a new boat and immediately started winning races. Therefore any fool can plainly see that the new boat is a hot one—particularly since it is now beating other boats from the same builder.

The answer to this is, to paraphrase a statement of Charles Kettering's, that the trouble with the skippers jumping to this conclusion is not that they do not know enough, but that they know too many things that are not so. They are probably ignoring the fact that this skipper has good sails, does a good job of sailing, and that anyone else probably would not have finished before dark with the boat he was using before he got the new one.

Another favorite example of these skippers is to point out that a certain boat always does well (or badly) under some particular condition, such as in a very light or very high wind, and the assumption is that this is due to something mysterious about the lines of the boat. The fallacy here is that they are not separating out the important from the unimportant and are taking a supposition for a fact. The fact that the boat consistently wins (or loses) under certain conditions must be accepted as a fact—but the cause may be that the skipper has good sails for only one range of wind velocities, the skipper may be a good light-wind skipper and not know how to handle a boat in high winds (or vice versa), or any one of a number of other things which I hope will become apparent after reading this book.

However, between boats built to identical measurements, there are many things which make the difference between a good racing boat and a clunker, and a tremendous difference in performance can and does exist between boats with identical lines. But none of these things are mysterious and there is no reason why anyone, particularly if he is starting out with a new boat or has an old one which is not in too hopeless a condition, cannot have one which is as good as the best. The best boat is the one on which the owner has done the best job of doing *all* the things that help to make a good boat. Tuning up a boat really involves doing all these things—there isn't any such thing as tuning up a boat to make it a winner by a few minor adjustments. These adjustments are only the finishing touches that are put on after a lot of work.

No attempt will be made here to tell how to build a boat—there are plenty of books on that subject, and the various classes have their plans and instruction books. I will only stress those items that are important in making your boat equal to the best. Many of them will be small, but they are the things that make the difference between an outstanding boat and just a good boat. Very few single things will mean much—it is the cumulative effect of lots of small things that counts.

allows if you can carry the maximum weight board and still have a minimum weight boat and unless your wife or girl friend or small child crews for you. In these cases, use a lighter board and lean out farther. More on this later.

Aluminum alloy is satisfactory for most parts and will save a great amount of weight as compared with brass parts; however, for use around salt water, aluminum is not satisfactory for parts which are in contact with bronze or stainless steel.

When aluminum and bronze or stainless steel are in contact in the presence of salt water they set up shop as a battery-charging station because of the difference in their ranking on the electrolytic scale. The aluminum suffers corrosion in the process; and especially in the case of aluminum nuts used on stainless steel bolts, intergranular corrosion of the aluminum develops. The result is that the nut splits in half, and in one very unhappy case that I had some personal experience with in the Snipe National Championships in 1948, the bolt came out. Since that bolt happened to be the one holding my tiller onto the rudder, and since the wind was blowing about 30 miles an hour, I did a couple of fast whirling-dervish maneuvers before getting out the anchor; and the fact that I made a baling wire repair and finished the race was of academic interest only. My only consolation was that a Navy launch on which my wife had bummed a ride lost its rudder control too, and was towed in ignominiously by the harbor master.

Later I found an aluminum slide, which was on a stainless steel track on the side of the centerboard trunk, split the whole length of one side. From these experiences I recommend never having aluminum in contact with either bronze or stainless steel. The experts will all tell you that this is not true in the case of stainless steel, but I can't agree.

Aluminum bolts and screws are now available in many hardware stores, and bolts may be made by threading aluminum rod. Aluminum nuts may be purchased from any aircraft supply house and from many airports and hardware stores.

Aluminum is easy to work in a home shop with hand tools, and so much weight can be saved by its use that it should be used wherever possible. Parts may either be cut out of sheet or bar by sawing and filing, or bronze parts may be used as a pattern to produce aluminum castings. Aluminum castings should not be used for highly stressed parts unless they are produced with a control of foundry technique and material not normally available. Cam action jam cleats, however, are a specific item that can be easily cast in aluminum, using the parts of a bronze cleat for a pattern for casting the dogs and using aluminum sheet for the base.

7

A power jig saw is handy for anyone making his own hardware. The regular wood-working blades work fairly well on aluminum, but a better blade can be made from a remnant of ribbon from a Doall saw. All tool shops have these saws and will have remnants of blade material left, as they purchase the material in rolls. One-fourth inch wide, 32-pitch blades are best for steel or hard bronze, and 18-pitch for aluminum or wood. In order to have much success in sawing stainless steel, it will be necessary to use idler pulleys to slow down the speed of the saw to about one-third the normal speed. Sears and Montgomery Ward also have metal-cutting blades, but the cast-off Doall blades are the best.

If you don't have room to have a workshop, you can mount your power tools on tables with casters on them and use them in the garage. Very good casters on which the wheels can be locked to prevent the table rolling around can be bought from any Maytag washing machine dealer for about 60 cents. Roll the tools against the wall when you put the car away. Of course this means leaving the car out when working on the boat, but if you care more for your car than for your boat, you will never be a good racing skipper. (It may take awhile to educate your wife to this viewpoint.)

Figure 1 shows a Sears Roebuck drill press mounted on an individual stand, and a Sears jig saw and Montgomery Ward table saw mounted together on one stand so that a single motor drives either saw. Both the jig saw and the drill press are fitted with idler pulleys to reduce the speed for working with stainless steel, and the stands are on casters so they can be rolled against the wall. Less space would be required by mounting the saws on separate stands.

It is impossible to keep a smooth finish on a boat with caulked seams. On small boats, all seams should be glued with waterproof resin glue. If the boat is built for caulked seams, take a portable router or a portable rotary saw and clean out the seams for from one-third to one-half of the thickness of the plank, and glue in a piece of wood. (Figure 2)

After this is done the seams should be taped on the outside either with aircraft fabric tape doped on or glass cloth tape set in epoxy or polyester resin. The tape will prevent the seams from opening up when the boat dries out, and the piece of wood which has been glued in will eliminate trouble with caulking pushing out as the boat takes on moisture.

Any projection or roughness under water will produce drag. The rudder and the centerboard or keel should be sharpened as much as the class restrictions will allow. Both edges of the centerboard should be so sharp that they will cut you if you do not wear gloves when handling it. The slot around

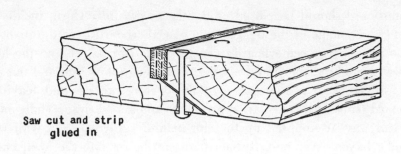

Saw cut and strip
glued in

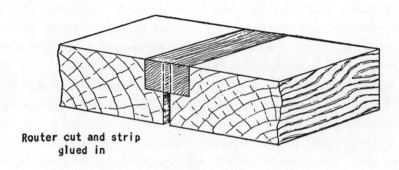

Router cut and strip
glued in

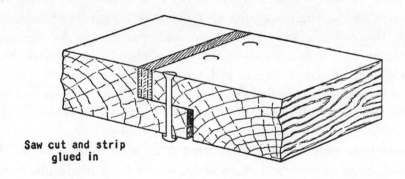

Saw cut and strip
glued in

Fig. 2

On small boats having caulked seams,
they should be reworked as shown above
to permit getting a smooth bottom.

the centerboard should be closed as tightly as possible. Here, incidentally, is the only advantage of the dagger-type of centerboard over the pivot type. With the dagger-type centerboard, a metal plate can be set into the keel to fit tightly around the board and not permit water to flow into and out of the centerboard trunk. The turbulence of this water entering and leaving the centerboard trunk will cause an appreciable amount of drag. There may be a practical way of stopping up the slot behind a pivot board with rubber flaps, but I haven't seen one. Rubber flaps can be set into the keel, but they don't do too good a job and cause jamming. *There must be no rough seams, gouges, or projections on the boat anywhere below the water line.*

For racing a small sailboat under all kinds of conditions, the cockpit should be smaller than is convenient for just ordinary sailing in order to keep the boat as dry as possible with high winds and waves. Also, with a small cockpit it is frequently possible to have a boat capsize and then be righted again without swamping, whereas this is impossible with a large cockpit. Large spray rails help greatly, but under extreme conditions a large amount of heavy spray will be thrown high in the air, and a fair amount of this eventually gets into the cockpit. I have seen the mainsail on a Snipe wet up to above the numbers, and after trying several different cockpit sizes on Snipes, I have settled on one four feet long and 21 inches wide, the forward end of the cockpit being 81 inches behind the stem. Attempting to keep water out by shortening the cockpit at its forward end is a serious mistake. This either results in the skipper and crew moving too far back for proper balance, or makes the crew slide back and forth on the deck which is extremely difficult. Of course in a dinghy or any class where the cockpit size is fixed, nothing can be done about this. Building in a self-bailing cockpit liner will help a lot in getting rid of the water taken on in heavy going, and permit the use of a larger and more convenient cockpit.

A very light and neat rubber extruded sheer molding is available. It has been used by many people with good success, and by many others with a distinct lack of success. The troubles experienced are from two sources—stretching the molding when it is applied, and not getting a good cement job. The molding should not be stretched at all when it is applied, or it will tear and come off as a result of a small gouge. The directions furnished with the kit will give a good cementing job, but most people do not let the cement dry enough before trying to apply the rubber strip. The cement should be dry enough so that it has just ceased to be tacky to the touch. If it is still even slightly damp, the rubber will not stick. Goodyear Pliobond is the best rubber cement I have found. It isn't as difficult to use as others I have tried.

3. The Finish of the Hull

THE FINISH OF THE HULL MUST BE ABSOLUTELY SMOOTH. THE SURFACE OF the wood must be smooth in the first place, with any rough spots being filled in with quick-drying hard putty. A relatively small amount of effort expended in sanding the wood will save a much greater amount of work later on. Duratite white putty is satisfactory for large gouges but does not seem to stay well in small ones. Z-Spar has a gray putty which is excellent for small gouges. These materials will shrink somewhat on drying, so large holes will have to be filled in several installments. There are also a number of automobile glazing putties which I have used. All of them are satisfactory, although some shrink more than others. All of the putties I have used are lacquer-base putties, but I have never had any trouble using them on enamel. I tried some oil-base putty once and got into a horrible mess. I had the stuff all over a boat before I discovered that it wouldn't dry in less than about three days' time, and when it did it wouldn't stay put. Plastic wood is not satisfactory as it expands and contracts too much with changes in moisture content.

My preferred method of building up a wood surface is to first apply two coats of sealer or thinned varnish. Any glued seams should then be taped with pinked-edge aircraft fabric tape doped on a fiberglas tape set in resin. The surface of the fabric tape should be built up with about six coats of clear dope and about four coats of aluminum pigmented dope (four ounces of aluminum paste to one gallon of clear dope). The tape should be sanded dry with No. 280 paper after each coat of clear dope. The aluminum dope should be sanded wet. On boats which are not left in the water, or which can be scrubbed every week, the surface of the bottom and top sides should then be built up with a flat marine enamel, wet sanding thoroughly after each coat with No. 320 paper over a rubber block. The number of coats required will depend on the smoothness of the original wood surface. The last two coats should be a gloss enamel, wet sanded after each coat with No. 400 paper by hand — do not use the rubber block. If fouling conditions are bad, an anti-fouling bottom paint must be used on the bottom if the boat is left in the water. Coperoyd can be sanded to a smooth finish and does a good job of preventing fouling.

Getting a smooth surface will be much easier if the paint is sprayed on. This can be done either by renting a spray outfit, hiring a painter who has one, or taking the boat to an automobile paint shop. It may be easier to do your own spraying of marine enamel or anti-fouling bottom paint than to convince a professional that the stuff doesn't work like car enamel. Marine enamel and anti-fouling bottom paint must be sprayed with as little thinner as possible, and each coat must be light. Pouring the paint on heavy will not only result in runs, but you may also get a wrinkled effect from the surface drying so fast that the solvents underneath cannot get out. It helps to hold the gun a little farther away from the surface than with car enamels, and do not try to accelerate the drying with heat—sometimes it works, but more often it results in a wrinkled finish, or even blisters.

For the last few years, I have been using automobile refinish enamel. It comes in all colors of the rainbow, and seems to stand up quite well—at least on a small boat that gets beaten and bashed up enough so that it has to be repainted every year. It sprays very easily, and if you are in a hurry or do not have facilities for spraying, you can get the job done quickly and cheaply by an automobile paint shop. If the job is done well, you may not even need to sand it.

In refinishing a boat, do not use paint remover unless the old finish is very bad. Paint remover gets into cracks and seams and is hard to get out. Wet sanding with No. 180 paper over a rubber block takes a lot longer, but it will produce a better final result. Paint can also be burned off, but this is risky business for an amateur. After filling all gouges with putty, sand until a smooth finish is secured or until as much of the old paint is removed as is desirable from a standpoint of weight removing. In refinishing over an old surface that is good, you generally can use only gloss enamel without the flat undercoat. If you have ever used a polish or a wax with a silicone base, this must be completely removed by sanding and washing with a solvent, or your new paint job will be the weirdest thing you ever saw. The important thing to remember is that it is not the paint that is put on that makes a smooth job; it is the paint that is sanded off that counts.

Covering the entire boat with light cotton fabric doped on, or thin glass cloth set in epoxy or polyester resin is very effective in preventing splitting and checking, which occurs frequently in cedar planks or in the outer plies of fir plywood. Many people think that they can get a smoother finish with the fabric covering than without it. This is not true, as any imperfection in the wood will show up after the fabric is put on. The only advantages of fabric covering are that it stops splitting and checking of the planking, it reduces the damage caused by the inevitable bashing of the topsides which occurs while racing or when a number of boats are tied to a float, and the dope dries well in damp weather which may be a help when trying to apply a finish in the spring. This method of finishing will weigh about seven or eight pounds more than an enamel finish over the bare wood with taped seams on a boat the size of a Snipe if aircraft fabric is used. Glass cloth will add about twenty pounds.

When using cotton fabric and dope, any old paint must be removed down to the bare wood. Apply two coats of sealer or thinned varnish to the bare wood and let them dry thoroughly. Then lay on the fabric like you would put on wallpaper, covering a section of the boat about two feet long with clear dope, pressing down the fabric, and then putting a coat of dope on top. Don't try to use too wide a piece of cloth or you will get into trouble. Use separate strips from the center of the keel to the chine, from the chine to the sheer, for the transom, and for each side of the deck. Also, borrow your wife's ironing board and iron out any wrinkles in the cloth before putting it on the boat. If you don't, wrinkles will still show after doping. The dope should be slapped on liberally, and all air bubbles should be worked out by hand. This leaves your hands in an awful mess, but lacquer thinner will take most of the caked dope off your hands, and the rest will wear off eventually.

If bubbles appear after the first coat, they may be worked out the same way or by splitting them with a razor blade to get the dope underneath. A particularly obstinate bubble which shows up after several coats of dope have been put on may be cured by purchasing a hypodermic needle at the drug store and squirting dope under the fabric. If you get absent-minded and let the dope dry in the gadget, you are out of luck. Clean the needle with thinner after about two fillings of dope.

Where two pieces of fabric come together, trim them so that they do not overlap, and then dope on pinked-edge tape. Airplane tape, light-plane grade, is the easiest to use, although you can make your own from cotton fabric and pinking shears. Where the fabric is due to stop, such as at the sheer with a varnished deck, the fabric should be trimmed a little short and the job finished with a pinked-edge tape doped on.

The edge of the fabric itself can be pinked but this is usually difficult to do, and it is easier to trim the fabric roughly with a razor blade and then dope on the tape, getting the edge exactly where you want it. Tape should be at least $1\frac{1}{2}$ inches wide, with the fabric trimmed back to give about $\frac{3}{4}$-inch overlap of the tape over the fabric. Tapes should be put on after the first coat of dope has dried on the fabric.

The number of coats of dope required will depend on the smoothness desired. Of course more dope must be used for the topsides and bottom than on the deck in order to achieve the desired finish. The clear dope may be put on easily with a brush, as it may be literally slopped on and still have a smooth finish. After the first two coats, the clear dope may be sprayed if desired. Clear dope should be used until the fabric is fairly well filled— probably about six coats on the topsides and bottom. Two or three are enough on the deck. All of this may be put on in a few hours, as the dope dries rapidly. Sand lightly, dry, with No. 280 paper between coats on the topsides and bottom. Do not sand the deck.

The deck can be given a final coat either of enamel or of pigmented dope; one coat is sufficient. A deck finished with dope and only one coat of enamel will probably be fairly rough; it may be made more skid-proof by sprinkling sander dust on it from a cheesecloth sack. Sawdust is too coarse and will wear out your pants in no time at all—dust from sanding is very good. It should be sprinkled on the next-to-last coat of dope or paint while the dope or paint is wet.

On the topsides and bottom, aluminum pigmented dope (four ounces of aluminum paste in one gallon of clear dope) should be put on after the clear dope. This may be brushed on or sprayed, but spraying is best. If it is sprayed, thin only enough so it will go through the gun, and the dope will dry just about as fast as it is sprayed on. About four coats will be required, wet sanding lightly between coats with No. 280 paper and a rubber block. Use No. 320 paper after the last coat. By putting on enough aluminum dope before starting the enamel, all signs of the cloth will disappear. The pinked edges of tapes can be hidden by spreading glazing putty along the edge with a putty knife and sanding. Care must be taken not to sand all the way to the cloth fibers after the last coat of dope, as the enamel will not cover satisfactorily over bare cloth. If you do this, put on a little clear dope and sand very lightly before putting on the enamel. If you don't notice it until after the enamel is on, use glazing putty.

Kits complete with glass cloth, resin and instructions are available from many sources. The glass cloth covering is much stronger than cotton fabric,

14

but heavier and harder to finish.

Finish with two coats of enamel or one coat of anti-fouling paint, wet sanding without a block with No. 400 paper between coats. The drying time before sanding the enamel will vary greatly with the temperature and thickness of the enamel but will generally not be less than 24 hours and may be over 48. Do not rush the final sanding—and be careful of all corners—it is easy to go through and impossible to do a perfect job of touching up, as the spot will almost always show.

The best finish will be secured by polishing with rubbing compound (available at any auto paint shop), but this should not be attempted until the paint has set a month, as the solvent in the compound sometimes softens new paint. An earlier polish job with Duco No. 7 polish is satisfactory, but the job will not be quite as good as compounding. Never try compound or polish on any copper-bottom paint—there may be some compounds and polishes and some copper paints that will work together, but all that I have tried result in the solvent in the compound dissolving the copper paint, no matter how long it has been on.

All of the foregoing instructions are on the assumption that you want, and can take care of, a finish that is the ultimate in making the boat go fast. If you have to leave your boat in water that is exceptionally dirty, where fouling conditions are particularly bad, and if you can't scrub the boat frequently, you may not want this type of finish. If this is the case, you will want to use one of the softer paints which keeps itself clean by slowly sloughing its surface. This type of paint is available for topsides and also in anti-fouling varieties for bottom paint. You will not get as smooth a finish with this material, but if everyone in your locality uses it and you don't care about racing in other places, you are all right.

The degree to which aluminum parts must be protected depends on the amount of time that the boat will be exposed to salt water. The best protection is given by anodizing or alumiliting, followed by a thin coat of zinc chromate primer and enamel. For only occasional exposure to salt water, clear spar varnish will give satisfactory protection without either alumiliting or anodizing.

Alumiliting and anodizing are electrolytic processes for producing an artificial oxide surface on the aluminum. This surface is fairly resistant to corrosion itself and founds a good base for paint. Many commercial electroplating plants have one process or the other. Bright colors can be produced by dyeing the surface after alumiliting. It is suggested that a plating company or an aluminum company be contacted for details on these processes.

4. Rigging the Boat

MOST BOATS WILL NOT BE PERFECTLY BALANCED UNDER ALL WIND VELOCI-
ties; a slight lee helm with a light wind will not do any harm, but carrying
the rudder deflected in a high wind to counteract weather helm will slow
down the boat by an appreciable amount. Therefore, the boat should be
rigged to have a slight lee helm in a light wind, if necessary, in order to
reduce as much as possible the weather helm which the boat will possess in
a high wind. This may generally be accomplished by rigging the mast as
far forward as possible and the centerboard as far back as possible. Moving
the jib stay back and forth has some effect on balance, but not nearly as much
as the location of the mast or centerboard. About ten years ago I made an
adjustable jib stay fitting for my Snipe to permit adjusting its location
between 11 inches and 19 inches behind the stem, intending to do a little
experimenting. The mechanics of the adjustable feature were not too good
and the thing always slid to $13\frac{1}{2}$ inches behind the stem. Since I was
winning races with it there, I gave up and left it there. The location hasn't
changed since.

With a pivot-type of centerboard, swinging the board back a little will
greatly reduce weather helm, and without the center of gravity of the board
being raised by an appreciable amount.

According to Manfred Curry's theories on the relative location of the
jib and main, the jib stay should be as far back as possible. Dr. Curry
conducted very extensive experiments on actual boats and on models of
sails. He arrived at a number of conclusions, most of which I think are
correct; however, there is one very unfortunate thing about the science of
aerodynamics and its practical application—whether to airplanes or to sails
—and that is that the air currents didn't go to college, they haven't read the
books, and they don't always do what the best aerodynamic theories say
they should. The aerodynamics engineers of aircraft companies have done

16

their best to educate these air currents by using exact scale power models in excellent wind tunnels, calculating results with slide rules, comptometers, IBM machines, and now even electronic calculators, but airflow remains illiterate—it still cannot read, and all theories must be modified by experience with the actual airplane or sailboat.

This probably sounds like rank heresy in a book on scientific sailing, but before jumping to this conclusion refer back to the definition of science in the introduction. Here is a typical case where it is necessary to be sure of your facts first, and then be sure that the conclusions at which you arrive are correct. It is also the first of numerous examples where an attempt to blindly apply principles of airplane aerodynamics to a sailboat will get you into trouble. Airplane wings and sails aren't the same—an airplane wing has two rigid surfaces, and a sail has a single flexible surface; their only similarity is that they both produce lift when the wind blows on them.

The accepted theory is that the jib and the main together work like a slotted wing on an airplane. I am convinced that the jib does not contribute anything to the efficiency of the main by the slot effect, and that its primary contribution is from the fact that it is in itself a very efficient sail without any mast to induce turbulent airflow right at the leading edge of the airfoil section. A slotted wing section produces high lift at high angles of attack, but also produces a high drag which results in a lower ratio of lift to drag with the slot open than with it closed. With a sail, we are working at as low an angle of attack as we can get, and we couldn't get a very efficient slot anyway even if we wanted it, because if we get the jib close enough to the main to accelerate the airflow the way it does with an airfoil slot, the main just collapses at the luff. This conception of how a jib functions, I believe, offers an explanation for some other differences of opinion which will come up later.

A forward rake on the mast will help to counteract weather helm, but the sails will set better in a light wind if the mast is raked slightly aft. The roach on the leech of the mainsail has a tendency to fall over in light air anyway, and any forward rake of the mast tends to make this worse. By raking the mast aft, the entire luff of the sail is supported by the bolt rope— not just hung from the headboard. I rig my Snipe mast so that the step is as far forward as the restrictions allow, and the mast is raked slightly aft when the jib stay is tight.

In small boats the side stays generally limit the amount that the jib can be trimmed in, yet it is desirable to have the side stays as far away from the mast as possible in order to cut down the compression load in the mast.

It is generally permissible to run the jib sheet inside of the stays; however, this is very inconvenient when shifting from a beat to a reach or a run, and the desired end can be accomplished by merely leaving the side stays slack. When the stays are slack, the mast should not be blocked where it goes through the deck. The hole should be large enough so that the mast never touches the sides of the hole. If you sail where there are big waves, you had better fit a rubber cover around this hole to keep water out.

When the boat is sailing, the stay on the windward side is automatically tight, and the stay on the leeward side is automatically loose. The luff of the jib and the jib stay are kept tight when on a beat by the pull from the mainsheet being transferred from the boom to the mainsail. As the boat goes from a beat to a reach and still farther out of the wind to a run, the load on the jib stay becomes progressively less. This is no disadvantage; in fact, when far enough off the wind to have the whisker pole out, it is an advantage. Of course, if the boat has a back stay, it keeps the jib stay tight all the time. When hoisting the sails at the dock with loose rigging, the jib halyard should be pulled up enough so that the jib stay is somewhat loose. This will insure having proper tension on the luff of the jib at all times.

The exact amount of slack in the stays does not seem to be important, but the stays should be much looser than one would think—particularly for a skipper accustomed to larger boats. The amount of slack in the stays on my Snipe has varied from 12 to 20 inches measured at a point 36 inches above the deck, with the stay being pulled tight enough in each direction so that all slack is taken out of the opposite stay and the jib stay (Figure 3).

With loose stays, universal joints should be used on the lower end of the turnbuckles so the stay will let the jib be trimmed in without bending the turnbuckle. On my Snipe I use $^3/_{32}$-inch diameter, 1 x 19 stainless steel cable with standard swaged end fittings. Ball and strap fittings are not completely dependable on 1 x 19 cable, especially if they are hand swaged. If the job is done properly with a power swager, they are safer, but a pulled off ball fitting cost me a National Championship once and I'm not about to experiment any further. No one else seems to have had this trouble, so they are probably all right. On the lower end I use a clevis-type fitting and a homemade universal joint, and on the upper end of the side stays, a clevis-type fitting which attaches to the mast tang. The mast tangs are attached to the mast with $^3/_{16}$ stainless steel rod threaded on both ends. One-fourth inch diameter steel bushings through the mast provide the necessary bearing area, and an aluminum strap picks up an additional bolt. The jib stay has a fork end swaged fitting on the top and is attached to a tang pinned into

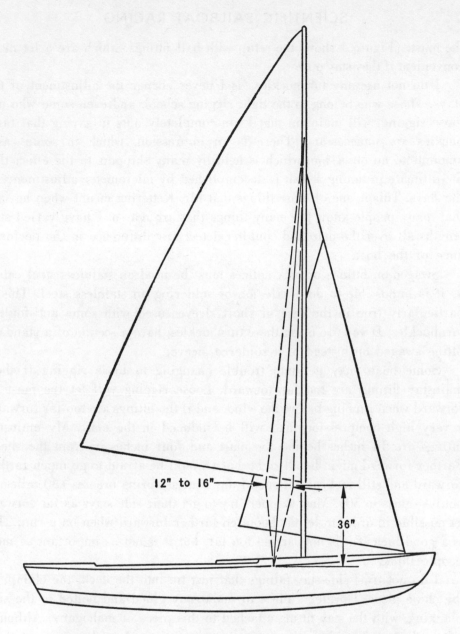

12" to 16"

36"

The jib stay should be adjusted so that when the slack is taken out of the side stays, the mast rakes aft slightly. The amount of slack in the side stays should be checked by alternately pushing and pulling on one side stay at a point 36 inches above the deck to take all the slack out of all the stays. The figures shown are about right for a snipe.

Fig. 3

the mast. (Figure 4 shows the setup with ball fittings, which are a lot more convenient if they stay on.)

I do not use any turnbuckles, as I never change the adjustment of the stays. Those who belong to the tight rigging school, and even some who use loose rigging, will maintain that I am completely nuts in saying that turnbuckles are unnecessary. There is an impression, which in some cases amounts to an obsession, which is held by many skippers to the effect that the ultimate in tuning a boat is accomplished by micrometer adjustments of the stays. This is one of those things that Mr. Kettering meant when he said that many people know too many things that are not so. I have varied stay lengths all over the map and couldn't detect any difference in the performance of the boat.

Swaged-on fittings or tuck splices must be used on stainless steel cable, as it is impossible to do a safe job of soldering on stainless steel. This is particularly true in the case of short sleeves used with some anti-fouling turnbuckles. If you are using these turnbuckles, have a section of a standard fitting swaged on instead of a soldered sleeve.

Some boats may get into trouble changing to loose rigging if their mainstay fittings are too far forward. Loose rigging will let the mast go forward when running before the wind, and if the fittings are too far forward, a very high compression load will be induced in the mast. My mainstay fittings are 14 inches behind the mast and four inches in from the sheer. Farther forward might be all right, but I would be afraid to go much farther forward and still feel safe in one of our Kansas spring breezes (30 miles an hours—gusts to 50). Most skippers try to get their side stays as far forward as possible in order to let the boom go farther forward when on a run. This is a good idea if it is not carried too far, but it is not as important as most people think.

I do not trust side-stay fittings that just tie into the deck, the clamp, or the chine piece. I prefer a piece of mahogany glued and bolted to the side planking, with the stay fitting attached to this piece of mahogany. Although I have had no trouble with aluminum stay fittings, I no longer trust them because of their intimate contact with the steel ends on the stays. I now use $3/32$-inch thick stainless steel straps. My jib stay fitting is a stainless steel strap going from the deck down to the stem, where it is fastened with two No. 11 screws $2\frac{1}{2}$ inches long.

Wire halyards are much superior to rope halyards, as they will maintain their tension. I use $\frac{1}{16}$, 7 x 7 stainless steel cable, with a standard ball end fitting where the halyard attaches to the sail. Do not use the more common type of swaged fitting without the ball on the end of any halyard where the fitting will get close to a pulley. If the sail can be pulled up high enough so that the fitting tries to go around the pulley, it of course won't be successful, and the result will be a sharp bend in the cable where it comes out of the swaged fitting. This will very shortly lead to a fatigue failure of the cable.

Wire halyards may be spliced to a piece of line which is wrapped around a cleat, but winches are much more satisfactory. If a winch is used, it is necessary to provide a means of attachment to the winch on the lower end of the halyard. This same gadget should also prevent the halyard from disappearing up the mast when the mast is unstepped. If clearance is provided in the mast, a standard ball may be swaged on the end of the halyard before it is pulled through the mast. If this is done, a washer may be slipped over the ball after the halyard is pulled through the mast and then bent to act as a safety.

Another satisfactory end fitting consists of a $\frac{1}{4}$-inch diameter bolt with a hole drilled through it to run the cable through and a nut and two washers to clamp down on the cable. Care must be used in locating the hole for the cable so it will not be cut when the nut is tightened. (Figure 5)

When putting wire halyards into a mast in which rope halyards have been used, make sure that the wire halyard cannot jump off the sheaves. A $\frac{1}{16}$-inch diameter cable does not need much room to slide down alongside a sheave, and if it ever does, the works are really scrambled. The sheaves should fit closely in the slots in the mast, and if the sheave projects very far into a hollow mast, metal plates should be used on each side of the sheave to keep the cable from jumping off. It is much easier to take proper precautions against the cable jumping off than it is to repair the damage after it has occurred—especially as it usually occurs when you are in a hurry and generally ruins the halyard.

With wire halyards it is necessary to be sure that the attachments of the halyards are sufficiently strong, particularly in the case of the jib halyard. If this halyard is set up tight at the dock, the load that it will be carrying will increase greatly when the boat is sailing and the downward pull on the mainsheet is transferred through the sail to the mast, tending to pull the mast aft.

It is difficult to get halyard winches that are not excessively heavy (and expensive) for small sailboats, but it is easy to make them. The winch shown in the photograph has a drum which was turned from aluminum bar on a lathe, but an equally good winch can be made by making a center drum of

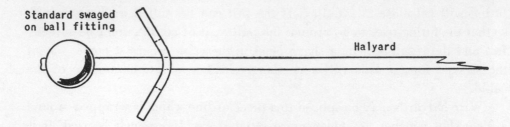

Standard swaged
on ball fitting

Halyard

Washer with hole just large enough
to slip over ball. After being bent
as shown, it will not slip back off.

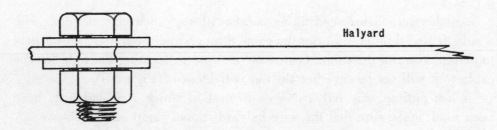

Halyard

Bolt with hole drilled through it 1/32-inch larger
than halyard. Locate hole so that when washers
tighten down on the cable, the cable will not be
cut by the edge of the hole in the bolt.

Fig. 5

If there is clearance in the mast to pull through the halyard with
a standard ball swaged to its lower end, use a washer as shown above to
keep the halyard from going back up the mast. If there is not enough
clearance for this, use the method shown in the lower illustration.
Standard ball fittings may be purchased for the upper end of the halyard.

22

FIG. 4

Standing rigging should be as light as possible, but strong enough to stand any conditions the boat may be subjected to. The stays and fittings shown are light, have a minimum of wind resistance, and have proved to have adequate strength.

FIG. 6

This halyard winch is made entirely of aluminum, except for the locking pawl which is stainless steel. The drum was turned on a lathe from bar stock. If you don't have a lathe, see Fig. 7.

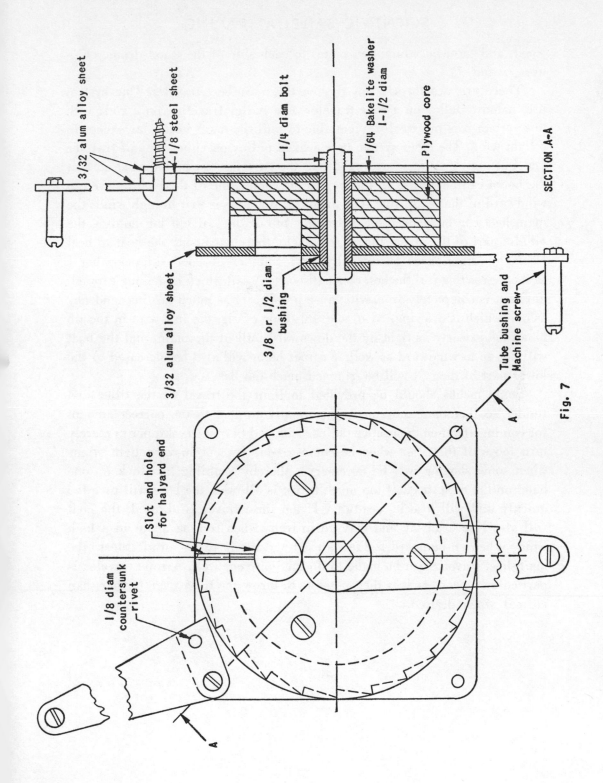

3/32 alum alloy sheet

1/8 steel sheet

1/4 diam bolt

1/64 Bakelite washer 1-1/2 diam

Plywood core

SECTION A-A

3/32 alum alloy sheet

3/8 or 1/2 diam. bushing

Tube bushing and Machine screw

Fig. 7

Slot and hole for halyard end

1/8 diam countersunk rivet

23

wood, and screwing aluminum plates to each side of the wood drum. (Figures 6 and 7)

There are two theories on rigging the mainsheet traveler. One system uses a loose pulley on a rope traveler or a pulley traveling on a rod; with this system it is practically impossible to pull the main in too far except in a light wind. The other system uses a fixed pulley on either type of traveler and in some cases is so arranged that the traveler can be adjusted so that the boom can be pulled all the way to the center line of the boat or even to windward of the center line. The theory of this type is that in high winds the mainsheet can be slacked off, letting the top of the sail luff but holding the middle part of the sail at the correct angle, thereby causing the boat to heel less. This rig is used successfully by a number of good skippers, but I cannot agree that it is the best on small boats. A sail which is shaking around, unless it is completely free, will cause practically as much heeling tendency as one which is drawing. Also, with this type of rig, the luff wire in the jib is not held nearly as tight by the downward pull of the main, and the boat will not go to windward as well. Weather helm will also be increased as the lower part of the sail will be trimmed much too flat.

Some means should be provided to limit the travel of the tiller and rudder so that their movement is normally limited to the correct amount for coming about on the proper radius. This will permit the skipper to merely turn loose of the tiller when he comes about (except in very light winds when some shoving will be necessary), thereby enabling him to keep one hand on the mainsheet. If too much travel is allowed, the boat will turn too quickly and will lose its headway. If too little travel is allowed, the boat will also lose headway and may go in irons when coming about in a high wind. When an outboard rudder is used and the boat has an afterdeck, the mainsheet traveler can be made to do this job very well. A rope traveler is particularly good, as it is then possible to throw the tiller over farther than normal when desired.

5. Boat Equipment

EVEN IF YOU HAVE ONLY ONE SUIT OF SAILS, FORE AND AFT ADJUSTMENT should be provided for the jib sheet fairleads. Also, it is desirable to have fairleads sliding on two tracks, one close to the sheer to give about a 14 to 15 degree angle between the tack of the jib and fairlead for use with full light-wind sails having a fairly flat cut jib and one farther inboard to give about an 11 to 12 degree angle between the tack of the jib and the fairlead for use with flat high-wind sails, any mainsail and a full cut jib, or any mainsail and any jib in a high wind. An intermediate adjustment between the inner and outer tracks would be desirable, as the 11 to 12 degree angle is pure guesswork. It seems to work and I have not tried any other position, but I still hope to find some good means of securing an intermediate position.

Probably the position for best efficiency is different with each suit of sails and involves a compromise between the disadvantage of backwinding the main with the jib trimmed too far inboard, and not being able to point as high with the jib trimmed too far outboard. The best solution is to let the main be backwinded slightly. This conclusion was originally based entirely on experience, but is supported by the theory that the chief contribution of the jib is to function as an efficient sail itself and not to control the airflow over the main.

Some people claim they can eliminate tracks by merely adjusting the position of the jib tack to give the proper direction of lead-off on the jib sheet. I do not agree with this, as it has been my experience that a small sailboat goes best to windward with the tack of the jib as close to the deck as possible, regardless of wind velocity or the sails used. Dr. Curry's theories do not support this, but I originally proved it to my own satisfaction by experience, and it now appears logical if my theory on how a jib works is correct. If the slot between the jib and main were of primary importance, the jib should be hoisted up until the foot is even with the boom. If the efficiency of the jib alone is important, it should be as low as possible. Also, as the wind picks up, the whole rig moves aft which means that the fairlead must be moved forward in high winds in order to trim the jib properly even when using the same sails as you use in light winds. My outer track is about two inches in from the sheer, and the inner one is eleven inches from the sheer. They are about 15 inches long, and their front end is 104 inches from the stem.

The tracks are bolted into a reinforcement of $\frac{1}{4}$-inch plywood below the deck, and this reinforcement and the deck in the vicinity of the track are well tied down to the deck beams. In a high wind there is a lot of load on the fairlead, and if the track pulls out the crew generally goes overboard and you have to fish him out, in addition to fixing the track before you finish the race.

Free-running blocks should be provided for all sheets, and there should be jam cleats both for the jib sheets and the mainsheet. Cam-action cleats which will hold or release the sheet in an instant are best. These cleats should be located where they can be easily reached at the time when they are needed most—which is on a beat in a high wind. The best location for the jib sheet cleats is on the back of the centerboard trunk.

The mainsheet may be led to a snatch block and cleated on the aft end of the centerboard trunk or on a cross member across the cockpit, or to an arrangement such as Lou Varalyay's "Louie post." Owen Duffy rigged up a jam cleat on a swivel attached to the boom. I had a similar arrangement at one time, but after being brained by it a couple of times while jibing, I took it off. It has the advantage of giving the skipper a better means of supporting himself when leaning out in a high wind, but at the same time it tends to pull the boom in fairly far. It is a bit difficult to use on a reach or a run, and sometimes is hard to release on a beat in a high wind. I prefer the location on the centerboard trunk on a Snipe, or on a cross member across the cockpit on a larger boat, as I leave the main cleated when I tack; and the mainsheet led to either of these locations does not interfere with handling the tiller. The cleat on the boom is simple and has become very popular. Just recently, a cleat to be attached to the rear of the centerboard trunk has become available in England and the United States. With either of these arrangements, the crew can help in trimming the main in a high wind or when rounding a mark off a run onto a beat, which is difficult with the "Louie post" arrangement.

All sheets should be big enough to permit getting a good hold on them, and it is desirable to use smaller sheets in light winds than in high winds. A wide range of sheet sizes should be provided for a spinnaker, ranging from marline or flag halyard on up. Light spinnaker sheets are especially important in light winds, as it is desirable to let the clew of the spinnaker float as high as possible. The sheets should attach to the spinnaker with swivel shackles so that the sheet will not twist the sail, and also these shackles should be large enough so that the snap shackle on the spinnaker pole can clip into them. Cotton sheets are easier on the hands than manila, and for that reason cotton is more desirable for the mainsheet and for jib sheets on high-wind sails. I use a $\frac{5}{16}$-inch mainsheet, $\frac{5}{16}$-inch jib sheets on high-wind sails and $\frac{1}{4}$-inch sheets on light-wind sails. All of them are cotton—a lighter mainsheet would be a definite advantage in light winds, but you never know when the wind is going to pick up. So far, I have just struggled along with the heavy one regardless of wind velocity. I have also experimented with various synthetic sheets. Soft woven nylon has worked well, but is very expensive. Dacron has worn out in no time at all. "Pimm" sheets are very good, but cannot be spliced. A further advantage of cotton sheets is that wet cotton sheets and wet cotton gloves have a very high coefficient of friction against each other, and therefore the sheets can be trimmed much easier in a high wind. Those of us who do nothing more arduous than pushing a pencil five days a week have trouble toughening up our hands, and this feature is a big help.

Good bailing equipment is essential for racing in a good breeze. Even on a small lake, you can take on lots of water in a high wind and on larger bodies of water you need the bailing equipment at much lower wind velocities. Until recently there hasn't been a good pump on the market and it has been necessary to build your own. The "Drain Buddy" mentioned in the earlier edition of this book was fine, but the book didn't come out soon enough—the company that had made it apparently folded up about the time the book was published. Recently a number of small boat skippers who have built their own pumps are starting to market them on a limited scale. I hope they are successful, as there is a real need for a good pump.

The "step-on-it" pump is completely inadequate for severe conditions, and seems to have a tendency to fall apart when most needed. Two of them can be rigged together with a walking beam arrangement and do a pretty good job if properly maintained, but many a race has been lost simply because of inadequate bailing equipment. It is also true, I am sure, that many skippers just simply don't go out when they think they may take on water. This is all right until you get to a regatta where the going is tough and there are properly equipped boats. In this case, unless you can rustle up some reasonably good bailing equipment, you might as well go home.

Some means of bailing on a beat is essential, preferably while hanging out balancing the boat. All of the good homemade pumps are rigged up to do this, and the new pumps now coming on the market can be rigged up easily to accomplish this.

The simplest, but least effective, way of bailing on a beat is with a kitchen pan with a long handle tied to a stick. It is at least better than nothing. An old-fashioned plunger type bilge pump will also do it, if it is large enough. It should be at least five feet long and two and one-half inches in diameter. It is inconvenient to use but will get the water out, and may keep you from a dunking. You should also have emergency equipment so that you can really bail if you need to. A gallon can, a wastebasket with a big handle on it, or a big bilge pump will do the job. In any case, have something that can be used while the boat is on a beat and while the skipper and crew are leaning out. Then you are not so likely to need the emergency equipment.

On a small boat the spray rails are just going along for the ride 99.9 percent of the time; however, when spray rails are needed, they are very essential, and it is better to have permanent spray rails on the boat which will take care of all but the most severe water conditions. These spray rails should be so installed that large emergency ones can be easily fastened to them if desired. The permanently installed spray rails should come out approximately to the stays and should clear the stays so that the emergency ones can come all the way to the sheer. I use spray rails five inches high, coming out to a point about even with the stays.

The tiller should be long enough so that the skipper can sit well forward. This should not be carried to extremes, however. One of the Snipes I sailed in the World's Championship races in 1949 had a tiller that was so long that I couldn't get in front of it without sitting on my crew's lap—I had to duck under. On one occasion I finished coming about with the tiller, the mainsheet and the jib sheet all wrapped around my neck. Fortunately I got myself untangled without capsizing or hitting anything. The tiller should also have a swiveling extension about 24 inches long so that the skipper can get out to balance the boat in high winds and still hang onto the tiller. The extension is also handy in getting farther forward in very light winds. The tiller on my Snipe is 63 inches long, measured from the forward edge of the rudder, and the extension is 24 inches long. I also have a piece of $1/4$-inch line about a foot long tied to the end of the extension.

On a long run before the wind, particularly in very light winds, some benefit may theoretically be gained by hoisting the entire jib as high as it will go so that its wind will be as free as possible. Whatever means are used for accomplishing this, however, must be foolproof, as any difficulty in getting the jib down where it belongs at the end of a run or if the wind shifts to a reach, will nullify any gain that might be picked up during the run. I have had my boat rigged this way but have never used the rig. On runs only a mile or so long, the risk of getting things scrambled up when going onto the next leg of the course or going onto a reach is so great that I don't think the theoretical gain is worth the risk. On longer courses it may be a different story.

The whisker pole should be long enough so that when it is set the jib is practically straight across the boat. It should have clips on the outer end of the pole, and there should be a loop in the jib sheet at the clew of the jib to hook these clips into. This arrangement is a big help in getting the pole set in high winds and also permits jibing on a run without the pole coming loose from the jib. The best way is to splice the sheet at the jib, leaving enough slack so that the whisker pole may be easily clipped to it. Usually I just tie a knot in both sheets, leaving slack for the end of the pole (Figure 11). The inner end of the pole should merely rest against the mast with a piece of rubber or something similar to keep it from sliding down—too much time is lost, especially in high winds, with any arrangement which requires hooking this end of the pole into a fitting on the mast.

A sliding fitting should be provided on a track on the front of the mast for the spinnaker pole to clip into, and locking snaps should be provided on both ends of the pole. These snaps will fit into the sliding fitting on the mast on one end, and into a shackle at the tack of the spinnaker on the other end. The slide should be easily adjustable throughout the range necessary to enable keeping the pole level. The snap on each end of the spinnaker pole should also be large enough so that the snap on the forward guy can be attached to the pole.

Sideways bending of a mast is undesirable under all conditions, and for this reason I prefer a round mast to a theoretically streamlined one. If the streamlined mast were permitted to rotate so that it lined up with the sail, it would be fine; however, when the mast is fixed I believe a streamlined one has a higher drag than a round one, and a streamlined mast built to weigh the same as a round one will bend sideways much more than a round one— or conversely, a streamlined mast rigid enough not to bend laterally will be unnecessarily heavy.

On a small sailboat, any mast that is not excessively heavy will bend some in a fore-and-aft direction in a wind of around fifteen miles an hour or more. The amount of bending in any particular mast depends on where the side stays attach to the mast in relation to the location of the jib stay and jib halyard pulley, the type of mainsheet rig used, the fullness of the mainsail, how high the boom is carried, and how much the wind is blowing.

The amount of fore-and-aft bending will be increased rapidly by having the side stays intersect the mast above the jib stay. Conversely, if your mast is too flexible, putting the side stay intersection below the jib stay intersection will reduce the bending. (The relative location of these intersections is closely regulated in some classes.) Some additional bending can be induced where desired by having the jib halyard pulley some distance below the jib stay. If you want more fore-and-aft bending in your mast, this is a very good way to get it as the amount of bending induced is less affected by increasing wind velocity. This is because as the wind increases and therefore the downward pull on the boom from the mainsheet increases, the load to be carried between the jib stay and jib halyard and jib luff increases. The halyard and jib luff stretch easier than the jib stay, so the percentage of load carried by the jib stay increases and the percentage carried by the halyard, which is tending to cause bending in the mast, decreases.

Moving the mainsheet traveler forward will increase fore-and-aft bending of the mast, as will cleating the mainsheet so that it slopes forward as it comes down from the boom. The mast will also bend much more with a full mainsail, and the higher the boom is the more the mast will bend.

In some classes, such as the Star, very fancy rigs are used to facilitate bending the mast without waiting for the wind to do it. These classes also generally have means of bending the boom, both bending it downward in the middle and also sideways.

The merits of bending masts and bending booms will be taken up later in the discussion on sails, as the only reason for wanting a mast or boom to bend or not bend is because of the effect of this bending on the sails.

Regardless of the type of mast used, it should be hollow, if permitted in the class rules. It should be as light as possible and still be strong enough to stay put in high winds and with certain cuts of synthetic sails, stiff enough to keep the mainsail functioning in a high wind. Halyards should be led down inside the mast, as they will offer an appreciable amount of air resistance if led down outside the mast and will also greatly increase the turbulence of the airflow over the mainsail. If you have to have the halyards outside the mast, lead them down the front of the mast as close together and as close to the mast as possible.

Masts and booms should be slotted for bolt ropes on the sails unless

FIG. 8

Reading from top to bottom, the jam cleats are for the boom jack, the starboard jib sheet, the port jib sheet, either jib sheet when on a reach or a run and the centerboard is up, and the mainsheet. Also shown are the strap on top of the centerboard for the crew to hook his feet under and also incidentally to lift the board, the strap across the cockpit for the skipper to hook his feet under, and the line by which the bilge pump is worked on a beat (see Fig. 10).

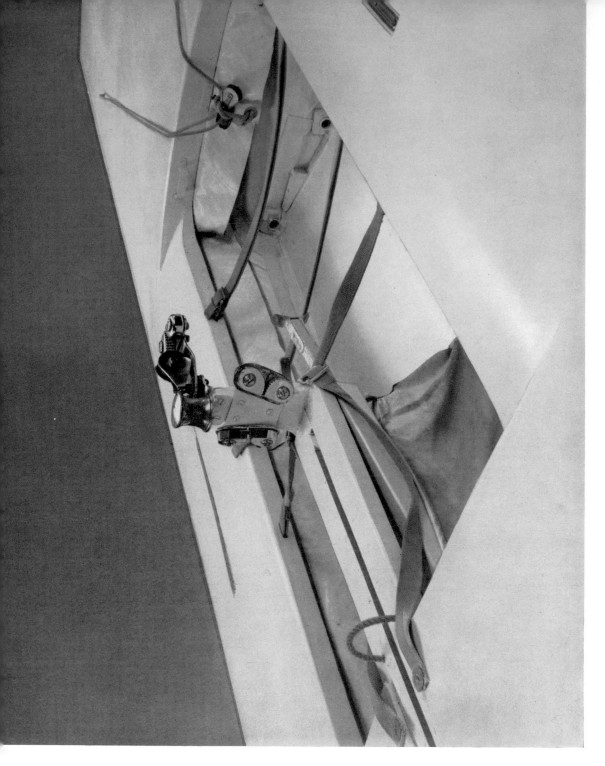

FIG. 9

The latest arrangement of hiking straps, jib sheet jam cleats, a jib sheet snubbing winch for use on reaches, and the mainsheet jam cleat is shown here. Note also the end of the whisker pole stowed in a tube alongside of the centerboard —an excellent arrangement with a self-bailing cockpit.

FIG. 10

The "Drain Buddy" pump shown here is no longer available, but a number of skippers have built similar pumps of their own, and this photograph shows a good method of hooking up any similar pump. This pump can be operated by foot when at the dock or when running before the wind, or by pulling on a piece of line when the crew is hanging out going to windward.

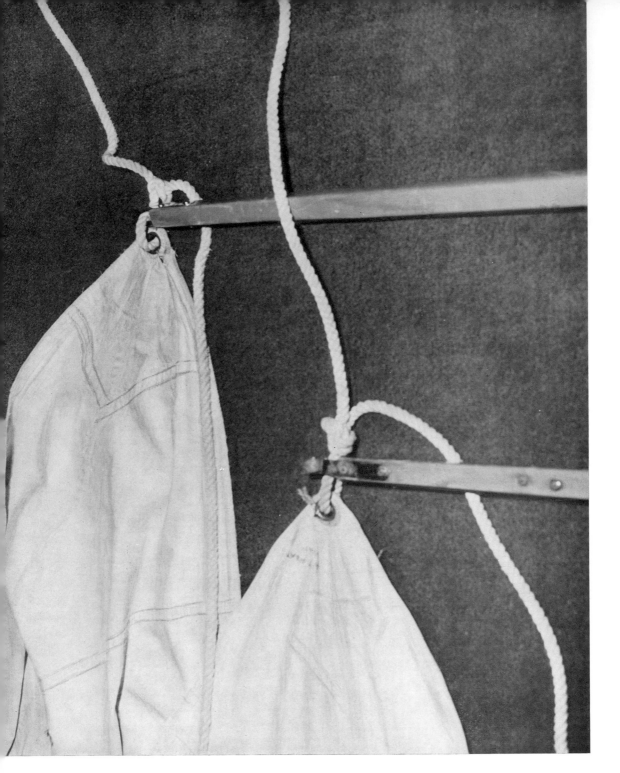

FIG. 11

Spring clips on the end of the whisker pole clipping into a loop made in the jib sheet by either a splice or a knot in the sheet make the handling of the pole much easier, especially in a high wind and when jibing while running before the wind.

FIG. 12

The leeward boat is in the process of passing 6025 because of difficulties experienced with the boom jack and whisker pole. Art Lippitt, my crew, is down in the cockpit because he is bailing—not to reduce wind resistance. We are both too far aft because the front of the cockpit is too far aft.

FIG. 13

The boom jack is shown here pulled tight to hold the boom down. The retracting mechanism, which is ¼-inch diameter rubber shock cord stretches out as the boom jack, which is ¼-inch cotton line, is pulled on. The line leads through a cam action jam cleat and then through a smooth cast pad eye so that it can be pulled on from any direction and locks itself automatically.

FIG. 14

The boom jack is shown here in the retracted position. To release the boom jack, it is only necessary to lift up on the line just behind the cam action jam cleat, and the rubber shock cord snaps it up out of the way. The mysterious black thing on the mast is a compass. Also shown is the snatch block and cam action jam cleat for the mainsheet at the back of the centerboard trunk, and an ordinary jam cleat just ahead of it for the jib sheets when the centerboard is raised.

FIG. 15

In stiff competition, this Snipe skipper would be out of luck because of limitations placed on him by his boat.

FIG. 16

In this photograph, the race is over and the skipper is sitting farther back than he should, but many of the boat details that have been discussed show up well here. My crew, Charles Henry, is sitting where he belongs.

FIG. 17

This photograph is also included to show boat details, not how to sail. The jib should be on the opposite side when sailing as close to the wind as this.

prohibited by class rules. Sails attached to the mast or boom with slides on a track are very inefficient because of leakage of air at the mast and boom and also the track is heavy. Trouble is sometimes experienced in splitting of the material forming the slot at the end of the slot. This can be prevented easily by making the end of the slot of ash.

The fitting on the gooseneck to which the tack of the main is attached should be so located that the bolt ropes on both the luff and the foot line up perfectly with the slots in the mast and boom or with the sail slides. The set of many a good main has been if not ruined, at least not helped, by the tack being secured an inch or so out of its proper alignment.

A gadget should be used to hold the boom down when on a reach or a run, except in very light winds. Even then, this gadget will be desirable if the sea is choppy, or if there are power boats running around, in order to prevent the boom from banging around and shaking the sails. This gadget is variously called a boom vang, preventer, boom jack, and boom downhaul. The term "boom downhaul" is more properly applied to the means of pulling down the boom at the gooseneck; vang and preventer don't have any particular meaning; so I use boom jack. (In England it is a kicking strap.)

The boom jack should lead to a point either on the mast or the deck at the intersection of the mast with the deck, rather than straight down from the boom to the deck. The reason for this is that it is needed most in a high wind on a broad reach, and if it leads straight down to the deck the crew cannot get over to the low side to attach it. Also, in case a boom jack leading straight down to the deck is forgotten at a mark, attempting to round the mark with it on is a sure way of being blown onto the mark and getting put out of the race. If the boom jack leads to the mast or the center of the deck, all that will happen if it is forgotten is that the crew will get tangled up in it when you round the mark, and he probably will not forget it the next time. The dinghy sailors in England have recently started using double block boom jacks so that they can really strap things down for close reaching. They claim it is very effective.

Another disadvantage of the boom jack leading straight down to the deck is that it takes some time to rig it, and that time can be very critical. The photograph, Figure 12, illustrates this perfectly.

The windward Snipe is the one I drew for the last race in the World's Snipe Championship in 1949. Its features included, among others, jib sheet fairleads which couldn't be adjusted because the screws had been twisted off, their fixed location being about six inches too far in from the sheer and the same amount too far forward for the jib I was using; practically a total lack of cleats; a whisker pole that had to be tied to the mast with a piece of line (believe it or not—it is the truth); and last but foremost in this discussion, a boom jack which had to be fished out of the bilge when needed, clipped with considerable difficulty into the same pad eye which held the forward mainsheet block, then let through an eye on deck and tied down. The end of the line was badly frayed in the bargain, making the threading through the eye on deck somewhat of a problem also.

On rounding the first windward mark onto a broad reach, I had a slight lead on the Argentines. By the time we finally got the whisker pole tied onto the mast and the boom jack rigged, the Argentines were well on their way to passing us to leeward—which they are doing in the photograph. They picked up enough speed while we were floundering around that we couldn't hold them, and we were unable to catch them until the next boat.

The boom jack shown in the photographs, Figures 13 and 14, can be pulled on instantly, it cleats itself, and when released from the jam cleat, it retracts itself out of the way. The retracting mechanism is a piece of $\frac{1}{4}$-inch rubber cord which runs through a block at the front of the boom, and is attached to a metal ring or one of those glass rings used instead of pulleys on awnings. The lines from the mast to the boom run through this ring. When the boom jack is pulled on, the rubber cord stretches permitting the boom jack to pull down on the boom. You can keep this rigged until the last second at a mark as it retracts itself in no time.

On a boat having a permanent back stay, a boom jack rigged to the center of the boat can be left on when jibing in a very high wind, and it will prevent the boom flying up and possibly getting hooked on the back stay. As a matter of fact, I always leave the boom jack on when jibing in even a fairly light breeze, as it prevents "goose wing" jibes where the top of the sail stays on one tack and the rest of the sail goes on the other. When this happens you usually have a batten or two broken or lost, and may also have a ripped mainsail. Also this type of boom jack can be left on if you get caught in a luffing match and have to pull in on your mainsheet rapidly.

The only advantage of a boom jack rigged to the deck is that in a very light wind it will tend to hold the boom forward, resisting the tendency of the weight of the mainsheet to pull it aft. This tendency can be counteracted either by the crew pushing on the boom, or a simple forward guy can be rigged to hold it there. Usually if the wind is light enough to need this, it is going to shift in a few minutes anyway so the crew might as well hold the boom forward.

An extremely handy gadget to use in a very light wind when there is a heavy chop or there are lots of water skiers around is a piece of light line to tie between the mast and the leeward stay. This will greatly reduce the shaking of the sails and is a big help to your peace of mind even if it didn't help keep your boat going—which it does.

In the photograph, Figure 15, the skipper is working hard at sailing his Snipe—but against top-notch competition he would look like a slow freight racing the Twentieth Century Limited—and all because of his boat.

The front of his cockpit is too far aft, forcing him and his crew to sit too far back. He has nothing for either him or the crew to get their feet under, and therefore they can't get out and balance the boat. For this reason the boat is heeling too much, even if the top of the main is luffing—which in itself doesn't make him go any faster. Partly as a result of the boat heeling too much, he is carrying a lot of weather helm—but even if he had straps so he and the crew could get out and balance the boat, it wouldn't do much good as he doesn't have a tiller extension which would let him get out of the boat to balance it and still hold onto the tiller which would then be in the center of the boat.

He also has no boom jack (or if he does, it is probably one of those that must be rigged to the deck on the leeward side of the boat, and the wind is too high for the crew to be able to get it rigged), so the lower part of his main is working at much too flat an angle, which is inefficient as far as making the boat go fast, and is causing a lot of the weather helm which is very apparent from the position of the tiller.

The mainsheet traveler is apparently of the knotted variety which means that he can't trim his main flat enough when he gets onto a boat without pulling the boom in too far, and the stays are so tight that he won't be able to trim his jib flat enough on a beat either. There are no signs of any cleats for either the mainsheet or jib sheets which will also affect the efficiency with which the boat can be sailed on a beat.

All of which adds up to the fact that no matter how good his sails are and how good a hull he has, and no matter how good a skipper he is—he would be in a hopeless position trying to compete with properly equipped boats.

Every parent of course thinks his own child is the prettiest and never loses an opportunity to show it off, and I therefore hope I will be forgiven for referring you to Figures 16 and 17, which show my Snipe on a beat and also on a broad reach. Many of the details I have been talking about are evident in these two photographs.

After everything has been done to provide as good a boat as possible, about the only thing remaining to do as far as the boat goes is to be sure before each race that everything is working properly and that nothing is about to fall off or break and to scrub the bottom with Bab-O if the boat has been left in the water. The method of scrubbing will be determined by the size of the boat and the facilities available. A small centerboard boat may be easily heeled over at the dock and scrubbed from a dinghy or on the shore in shallow water. A larger boat may be heeled as much as possible by having some nonworking spectators sit on one side and having someone else pull on a halyard, while the bottom is scrubbed either by getting into the water or using a long handled scrub brush from a dinghy. Tying a piece of cork to the back of the brush will provide pressure. This method can also be used from inside the boat, without the dinghy.

A thorough inspection should be made for frayed lines or cables, loose nuts or screws, broken cotter pins, and for the proper functioning of all cleats, bailing equipment, and watches. Also, the mast, boom, and whisker pole should be checked to be sure that there are no splits starting and that there are no small compression breaks that might lead to failure in a high wind. It is an excellent idea, however, to provide a small canvas bag attached to one of the deck beams and carry two pairs of pliers, a screw driver, a knife, a piece of wire, and some small line in this bag. Baling wire repairs shouldn't be necessary, but they sometimes are. Battens occasionally pop out while milling around before the start, particularly in a high wind. Have an extra set in the boat.

6. The Sails

SINCE THE SAILS ARE YOUR ONLY MEANS OF PROPULSION, THEY ARE OBVIOUSLY of vital importance. If you are going to race at all seriously, there is no point in trying to save money by buying cheap sails. My old cotton Watts medium sails which I used in about everything from 1941 until synthetics retired them in 1954 were getting pretty thin and the last few years I used them I was more careful about getting caught in a good blow with them, but they went just as well as when they were new. In fact, I think they went better. They won two World Championships, three United States Championships, and one Western Hemisphere Championship for me, and in the championships that I didn't win, it was never the fault of the sails. The point is—sails last a long, long time—and spread over their lifetime, a few dollars more for the best is of no importance, and don't let anyone tell you you have to have new sails every few years to be competitive. My own opinion is that it takes a skipper about two years to learn how to get the most out of a new suit of sails. If you buy new ones every few years, you will never know where you are. There is no easier and cheaper way to make a boat go fast than to buy the best sails, take care of them, and use them a long time.

Cotton sails were beautiful things, and I hated to have to give them up, but I don't think there are any die hards left who aren't convinced that synthetics are faster. There are probably two reasons for this—they are slicker and in spite of their wrinkles, probably have less wind resistance than cotton, and they are absolutely impermeable to air. The amount of air that leaks through cotton fabric may be very slight, but it is apparently enough to make a difference. Some people have done quite well with a synthetic jib and cotton main—supporting my contention that the jib is a very efficient sail—but from now on, I'm sure everything will be synthetic. You can continue to use the old cottons when the competition isn't too tough, and in a drifting match I have a suspicion that cotton sails might even be superior to synthetics, but in an important regatta it is going to be a rare occasion when you see cotton sails near the front. One reason of course is that the skippers who are likely to be in front regardless of sails will be using synthetics because they are afraid not to.

One big advantage of synthetic sails is that a given suit of sails can be used efficiently over a much larger range of wind velocities than cotton sails. This is partly due to the fact that they do not stretch, and partly due to the fact that the wind slips off of them with less drag, and therefore less heeling tendency. This is a real break for the average skipper, as he can have just one suit of sails and compete effectively against people with any number of suits of sails, under practically all conditions. As a matter of fact he may be better off, as he will never have a chance to use extremely full sails and then have the wind come up, or put on small flat ones and have the wind drop.

I have never believed that it paid to try to use extremely baggy sails with an exaggerated amount of draft for light winds. It has been my experience that a full-sized sail with medium draft was just as good, if not better, in a very light wind, and far superior if the wind picked up at all. My old stand-by 1941 Watts medium main gradually changed shape over the years, until the draft was just about uniform throughout the sail, with the maximum draft in the center of the sail, instead of being at the luff. When I first advanced the theory that mainsails should be cut that way to begin with, no one agreed with me. Most sailmakers still don't—but some do, and their sails have won a lot of races.

The transition from a full to a medium to a medium flat to a flat mainsail is gradual, and what one sailmaker calls a full sail might be called a medium by another (or even by the same sailmaker a few months later). On the matter of locating the point of maximum draft, all the sails I have seen fall definitely either in the category of having it as far forward as possible, or in the center. No part way measures, and this seems to apply to jibs as well as mains.

One sailmaker gave me quite a bit of argument on this subject of draft, pointing out that a study of aerodynamics would show that airfoils for low speeds all had the maximum camber well forward. The reason why a light-wind main is better with the draft well aft is, I believe, because the jib back-winds any light-wind main to some degree, but this has less detrimental effect if the draft is farther back.

I believe that the theory that the jib and main function separately and do not behave as a slotted airfoil helps support my contention on where the draft should be on a mainsail. Having the maximum draft well forward on the main will theoretically create a more efficient slot—according to the aero-dynamics of airfoils—but actually what happens is that the main is back-winded more by the jib, requiring slacking off of the jib sheet, resulting in poorer progress to windward. With the draft farther back, the jib can be pulled in farther without excessive backwinding of the main.

A high-wind mainsail will be cut with less draft than a light-wind main, and the point of maximum draft should be farther forward, although even on high-wind sails I prefer the maximum draft farther back than most sail-makers and skippers do. High-wind sails may be cut to the maximum meas-urements or may be smaller, depending on the amount of wind for which they are cut.

Because of the fact that you can use more draft in a synthetic sail at higher wind velocities than you could with cotton, the behavior of the mast may become critical, especially if the maximum draft of your main is in the center. In this case, the mast must be quite stiff as any appreciable bending will cause the sail to flatten out near the luff, then fall off badly on the leach, no matter how tightly you trim the mainsheet. I have seen this get to the point where the whole main was waving like a flag. If the draft of the main is well forward, the mast can bend considerably more without hurting the shape of the mainsail—if it can do so without breaking.

At the present moment, after only two years' experience with synthetic sails, I feel that a mainsail with a medium amount of draft located in the center of the sail, full size, with about all the roach you can get on the leach without its collapsing in a light wind, and a good stiff mast is the best bet for one mainsail for anything from a drifting match up to a wind of about 25 or 30 miles an hour. It is probable that a main with the draft forward might be better near the top of this velocity range especially if the mast weren't stiff enough, but I feel that throughout most of the velocity range the main with the maximum draft in the center of the sail will be more efficient.

The main reason why this sail is more efficient is that the jib causes less interference with it, and there is no necessity to compromise the trim of the jib because of the main. With this type of main, you can use an extremely full cut jib, sheeted to a fairlead on a track well in from the sheer, which would be murder with a main with the draft forward. (I know—I tried it once in an important race. The less said about the results the better.) When you finally learn how to trim one of these full jibs, they are very good in light to medium winds, and if your crew is husky enough and heavy enough, you can use them in any wind velocity. Whether they are actually superior to a fairly flat jib with the draft in the center like the cotton jib I used to use, I am not sure. I think they are about on a par going to windward, but I think the full one is superior on a reach. The average skipper and crew will do better with a fairly flat jib from about twenty-five miles an hour up.

There is at this time still quite a bit of argument concerning the best material for synthetic sails. I personally can see no difference between orlon and dacron as far as their performance is concerned. Nylon, of course, is suitable only for spinnakers. Any synthetic will probably last longer than cotton, although they may have to be restitched here and there every few years, as the thread seems to give out fairly soon.

If you have more than one suit of sails, it will appear to you that much of the time you are using the wrong ones, and if you have only one suit of synthetics you will not often have to race where you will be at a disadvantage compared to boats carrying sails suited perfectly to the wind velocity. Full-draft, light-wind sails are generally most efficient in winds up to about 10 to 15 miles an hour depending on how full they are; if used in wind velocities too much above this the boat will tend to heel too much, it will have a bad weather helm, and it will be necessary to slack off the mainsheet.

Slacking off the main and permitting the sails to luff when the wind is too high for the sails you are using will tend to cause them to go out of shape, and the boat will not go to windward as well as it will with a main that can be sheeted in tightly. A mainsail which has the maximum measurements but with medium draft is generally good for wind velocities up to 25 or 30 miles an hour. For higher winds, the sail should be made flat and slightly smaller than the maximum permissible dimensions. Some high-wind sails have less roach on the leach especially near the top.

On some larger boats, such as the Star, very fancy rigs are used to permit bending the mast in a fore-and-aft direction to take curvature out of a sail. On small boats, any round or square mast will bend some in a fore-and-aft direction. Theoretically a large amount of fore-and-aft flexibility is an advantage in permitting a full sail to be carried with high wind velocities, and some people have had sails cut with greater roach on the luff to take advantage of this. From a practical standpoint, I feel that the actual increase in velocity which can be handled *efficiently* in this way is fairly small, and that too much bending of the mast produces wrinkles in the sail that cannot help but be a detriment. A special sail cut too full for a straight mast is a definite mistake unless artificial means are used for bending the mast, as otherwise the mast doesn't bend until the wind blows, and therefore it will be too full in light winds. The same comments apply to bending booms; and where roller reefing gear is not used, I would make the boom as deep as permitted

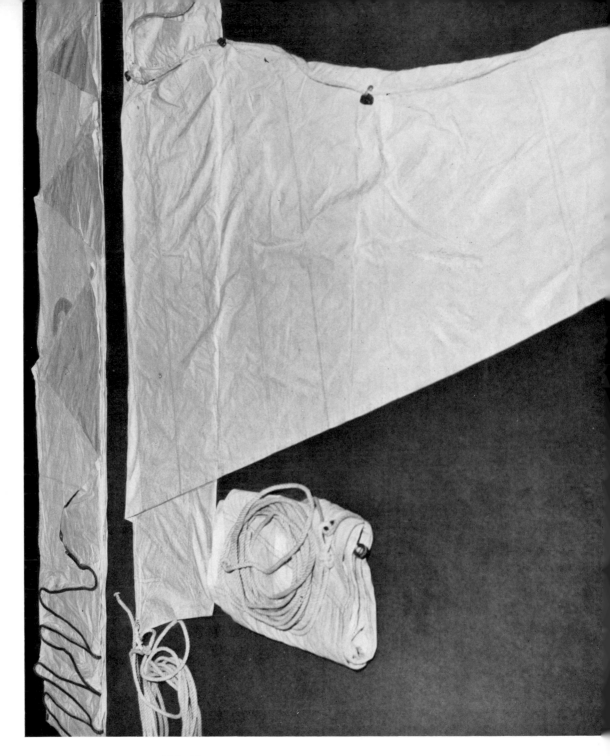

FIG. 18

A mainsail is shown here, on which the first folding has been completed with all folds parallel to the boat. One jib is shown partially folded and also another with the final rolling up completed.

as it is just that much more sail area.

I don't see any point in breaking in a synthetic sail in the same way that a cotton sail used to be broken in. The synthetic material has practically no stretch, and the sail should be ready to sail when you put it on the boat. The skipper however may need some breaking in to get accustomed to new sails. No two suits of sails, even of theoretically identical cuts from the same maker, ever behave exactly the same—especially jibs. I think that it takes a long time to become sufficiently familiar with a suit of sails to get the most out of them.

The fullness of mainsails may be varied slightly by pulling tighter on the luff and leech to flatten them out. The effect is slight, however, and much harm can be done by pulling sails too tight. If you should get caught with a flat main and a dying wind, lessening the tension on the luff and the foot will help put a little more draft into the sail and will be helpful.

Your boat should never be left at the dock with the sails up when there is an appreciable amount of wind. Allowing the sails to flap around in this way is bound to produce a loose leech and generally shake the sails out of shape. Drop your sails if you will be tied up more than just a minute or so.

I always fold my sails carefully and put them in a bag after drying them, even if I am going to use them the next day. Also, I fold them so that all sharp folds (and therefore the resulting wrinkles) are parallel to the foot of the sail (Figure 18). It may be silly to worry about the effect of a few wrinkles in the sail, but in my opinion this is just another one of those things which in themselves may have no measurable effect on the speed of a boat, but when many are combined may give you that one or two seconds a mile that you may need so badly.

In the last few years, some sailmakers have been making mitre cut mainsails for small boats. The theory is that in this way it is possible to avoid the flat spot that usually occurs for a little way up from the boom. This, of course, involves running a number of seams vertical where they will cause more drag and turbulent airflow over the sail. Some sailmakers say it is easier to make a mitre cut sail that sets perfectly while others say it is more difficult. I think you pay your money and take your choice. I know I'm not ready yet to toss out my old-fashioned two-year-old sails just because they aren't mitre cut. What I would do if I were buying new ones I am not sure—but I think I would take whatever the sailmaker recommended.

PART II

Getting the Most Out of Your Boat and Sails

I. Handling the Sails

THE PROBLEMS WHICH PLAGUE THE BEGINNER AND THE EXPERT ALIKE ARE: How close into the wind should I sail when going to windward? Where should I trim my sails? Where should my jib fairlead be? Don't let the experts kid you; they don't always do it right either, and two equally good skippers may have very different theories. To further confuse the problem, a good skipper may have different ideas at the end of each year; and for every theory why some things should work, there are equally good ones why they shouldn't work.

In general, sails should be trimmed as loosely as possible without the sail luffing when the boat is sailing on the desired course. On a beat, a jib which has a tight foot can be pulled in as flat as possible, and no harm will be done. A jib which has uniform fullness, however, must not be pulled in too tightly, particularly in light winds. Some curvature should remain in the foot so that the whole sail will not be too flat. An extremely full jib is particularly hard to handle, and is very sensitive to slight changes in trim. In a high wind it is generally physically impossible to trim the jib too flat; however, when the wind is variable, and it usually is, it will be necessary to slack off the jib sheet as the wind drops and pull it in again as the wind increases. The amount that the sheet is slacked off or trimmed in may be as little as $\frac{1}{4}$ inch, but that $\frac{1}{4}$ inch can make a real difference in the performance of the boat.

With a flat jib the jib fairlead should be farther out from the center line of the boat, especially if the main is cut so that the draft is well forward. The 14 to 15 degree angle mentioned earlier will generally result in putting the jib fairlead as close to the sheer as possible. Even with this location, a full or medium main will be backwinded some by the jib in any except very light winds. You cannot do anything about this, so just let the main go ahead and be backwinded. Flat sails, which should be used in a high wind, should have the jib fairlead closer to the center line of the boat on a line between the tack and the fairlead, making an angle with the center line of the boat of somewhere between 11 and 13 degrees. A full-cut jib must be trimmed well inboard at all times and will only work with a main with the maximum draft well aft. The trimming of a full-cut jib is an extremely tricky job, especially in light variable winds. The tendency is to trim it too lightly. As the length of the boat increases, these angles decrease. Ten degrees has been a standard number for large boats.

The fore-and-aft location of the jib fairlead should be determined by heading the boat into the wind slowly until the luff of the jib starts to shake. This shaking should take place simultaneously throught the entire length of the luff of the jib. With the fairlead too far back, the shaking will start at the top; with the fairlead too far forward, it will start at the bottom. Dr. Curry recommends intentionally carrying the fairlead a little aft so the leech of the jib won't backwind the main so much. It is my opinion that if any error exists in locating the fairlead, it should be in locating it too far aft, as this is far better than having it too far forward, but it should not be put far enough back so that the sail shakes appreciably sooner near the head. Do not try to locate your fairlead so the jib sheet is in line with the mitre of the sail—it is pure coincidence if the mitre and the sheet are in a straight line with the fairlead located properly.

On a beat the main should be trimmed so that the end of the boom is about halfway between the outer edge of the boat and the center line. This position will of course vary greatly with different types of boats and different sails, but the halfway position is a good place to start out. Most skippers make the mistake of trimming the main in too far, particularly in light winds. It is very easy to do this and you have to watch yourself constantly to keep from doing it. The mainsheet, like the jib sheet, needs to be watched continually in variable winds. If you cleat the main, you will have to adjust it frequently. If you don't cleat it, keep checking on yourself all the time— particularly if there are other boats close. There is an almost irresistible tendency to start trimming the sheets too tight when pressed by other boats. I trim my main so that the boom is in the same position regardless of wind velocity, until it becomes necessary to slack off to keep from heeling too much.

In order to understand the problems involved in trimming the mainsail, it will be a good idea to study Figure 19. The force acting on any airfoil may be considered as the resultant of the component of lift perpendicular to the chord line of the airfoil and of drag parallel to the chord line. (The

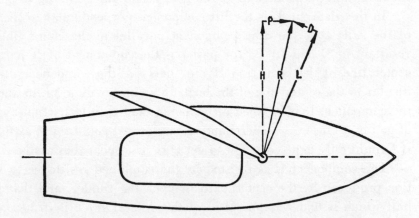

This diagram shows the forces acting on a sail with the wind
in the direction shown.

Wind

    L is the lift force on the sail, perpendicular to
      the chord line.

    D is the drag or resistance acting parallel to the
      chord line.

    R is the resultant of L and D.

    P is the component of R parallel to the boat cen-
      terline, which makes the boat go.

    H is the component of R perpendicular to the boat
      centerline, which makes the boat heel and also
      drift.

Fig. 19

chord line of an airfoil is a line going in the same general direction as the airfoil and is the line from which the airfoil is laid out. In the case of a sail, the chord line may be defined as a straight line connecting the luff and leech of the sail.) The resultant of these two forces may then be broken into a component parallel to the boat center line, tending to make it go forward, and perpendicular to the boat center line, tending to make it heel.

In the diagram, L is the lift component perpendicular to the chord line of the sail; D is the drag component parallel to the chord line; R is the resultant of D and L; P (for push) is the component of R parallel to the center line of the boat; and H (for heel) is the component of R perpendicular to the center line of the boat. In a similar diagram in another book, the component D is brushed off as being only a little friction and therefore of no importance. As an aeronautical engineer, I could retire awfully quickly if I could only figure out how to get D to disappear that easily.

The component H is resisted by the combined resistance to lateral motion produced by the centerboard or keel, the rudder, and that part of the hull which is under water. Most of this lateral force is of course supplied by the centerboard or keel. Since these surfaces are symmetrical, they must move through the water at a slight angle to provide the necessary force. This means that the boat will drift slightly to leeward at any time that the wind is not from directly astern. The amount of this leeward drift depends on the amount of surface on the centerboard or keel, rudder, and hull, and also on the shape of the hull. With most well-designed small racing sailboats the angle of drift is so small that it is seldom noticed. Normal inaccuracies in steering on a reach, and wind shifts on a beat affect the course more than drift.

Practically any racing skipper has at some time had the bright idea that if his centerboard could only be adjusted to make an angle to the center line of the boat, he could eliminate this drift and point better. This stunt would be prohibited in most one-design classes, and in any case I think its benefit would be doubtful. If the board could be made to turn without having any open places alongside the board for water to flow into the trunk, the boat might gain slightly, as a high aspect ratio surface (which the centerboard is by comparison with the hull) is inherently more efficient than a low aspect ratio one, and having the board pointed to windward just the right amount would make the hull go straight through the water. However, without a rather complex system of sliding seals, which would probably neither slide nor seal very well, it is necessary to have quite a wide opening in the keel for the centerboard, and this would probably cause more drag than would be saved.

From the diagram, Figure 19, it may be seen that trimming the sail closer to the center line of the boat permits the boat to head closer to the wind, but the force P becomes very small and eventually goes in reverse. By heading the boat farther out of the wind (assuming in all cases that the sail is trimmed to the point that it is just not quite luffing) the force P increases rapidly and the boat goes faster, but doesn't head as close into the wind.

Pointing a boat too closely into the wind is called pinching. The problem is: When are you pinching, and when aren't you? If a boat is pointed closer into the wind, it is on a better course and sails closer to the mark but makes less speed as shown in the preceding diagram. If it is pointed farther out of the wind it makes more speed, but the course is not as good. The problem arises in striking a happy medium. Pinching can be carried to such a degree that even the course achieved is not a good one, as the boat will lose enough speed so that it will slide sideways.

The effects of pinching or bearing off from the optimum heading are masked somewhat by the fact that the wind pennant shows the apparent wind direction, and this direction does not change as fast as the heading of the boat does. The apparent wind is the resultant of the actual wind direction and velocity and of the direction and velocity of the movement of the boat. If the boat is standing still, as it would be heading directly into a tide or river current whose speed was equal to the speed of the boat, the apparent wind and the actual wind would be from the same direction. As the speed of the boat increases, the difference between the direction and velocity of the apparent wind and the direction and velocity of the actual wind becomes greater. The sails are interested only in the apparent wind—they neither know nor care about the difference between apparent and actual wind. The skipper doesn't really need to bother about this difference either, as the actual wind is of academic interest only, but a knowledge of the relationship between the apparent and actual wind will help explain some situations that are confusing otherwise.

Different types of boats vary greatly in their ability to sail close to the wind. Large boats will generally sail closer to the wind than small ones; boats with a narrow beam will sail closer than those with a wide beam; and boats with tall masts and high aspect ratio sails will sail closer than those with shorter masts or gaff rigs. A representative number, which can be used for good small racing boats, is about 45 degrees out of the true wind.

Boats built to the same lines and having the same sails will all beat to windward best when the apparent wind is at the same angle to the center line of the boat. However, a faster boat will be farther off the actual wind than a slow one will when sailing at the same angle to the apparent wind. The illustration, Figure 20, is exaggerated somewhat, but it shows that with a fast boat you should not try to point as high as the slower ones, and with a slow boat you will go best to windward pointing a little higher than the faster boats.

The numerical values given in the diagram, Figure 21, are not intended to apply exactly to any boat and are merely illustrative of what happens when a boat pinches or bears off from the best sailing angle when on a beat.

It will be seen that while the angle to the apparent wind changes only about half as much as the angle to the true wind, the speed of the boat, especially when pinching, changes rapidly. This is like compound interest as each decrease in boat speed decreases the apparent wind velocity which further decreases boat speed. This is why it is hard to learn just when you are pinching and when you are not.

In light winds and no waves, the happy medium is generally just far enough off the wind so that the jib will not luff. When the wind varies from nothing to very little more, some skippers recommend bearing off as much as five or ten degrees farther off the wind than you normally would. I do not agree with this except in certain special circumstances which will be taken up later. With waves it is generally desirable to head the boat a little bit farther off the wind. The combination of a light to medium wind and a heavy chop is an extremely difficult one to handle, and takes a great deal of practice to master. Bearing off in this manner so as not to point so high in waves will seem to conflict with advice to be given later on the handling of a boat in high winds and big waves. This is another one of those cases where it is necessary to decide which of several factors is the most important in making the boat go fast, then doing the important thing and ignoring the unimportant—regardless of theory.

The technique of high-wind sailing will be covered separately later, but the change in technique with increasing wind and waves may be summarized as follows: In a light wind and no waves, point up into the wind until you are on the verge of luffing. With increasing waves, bear off a bit farther. Sail at this point until the wind becomes so high that in spite of getting out of the boat as far as possible, it heels too much. Then head into the wind enough so you can balance the boat until you approach the point of luffing. After that, slack off the main.

In connection with this problem of deciding how close into the wind you should sail, it will probably seem to you that every boat on the water is pointing higher than yours. Generally this is purely psychological; occasion-

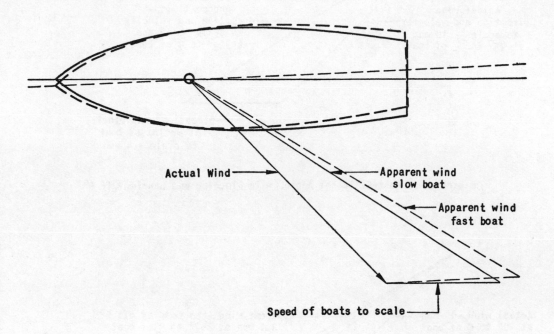

Actual Wind → Apparent wind slow boat

Apparent wind fast boat

Speed of boats to scale

The faster boat must sail farther off the true wind in order to keep the apparent wind at the correct angle to the sails.

Fig. 20

49

Boat Sailing with Wind at Correct Angle
for Most Efficient Progress to Windward

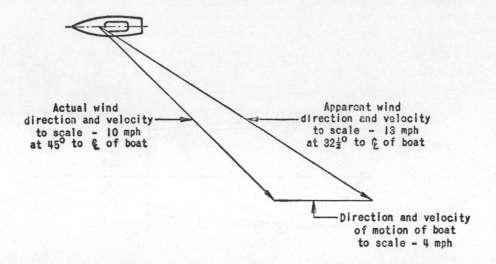

Actual wind
direction and velocity
to scale - 10 mph
at 45° to ₵ of boat

Apparent wind
direction and velocity
to scale - 13 mph
at 32½° to ₵ of boat

Direction and velocity
of motion of boat
to scale - 4 mph

Comparison of Most Efficient Angle, with Pinching and Bearing Off 5°

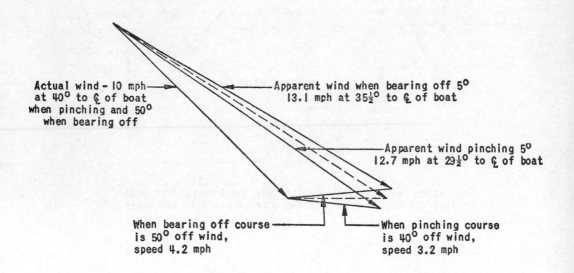

Actual wind - 10 mph
at 40° to ₵ of boat
when pinching and 50°
when bearing off

Apparent wind when bearing off 5°
13.1 mph at 35½° to ₵ of boat

Apparent wind pinching 5°
12.7 mph at 29½° to ₵ of boat

When bearing off course
is 50° off wind,
speed 4.2 mph

When pinching course
is 40° off wind,
speed 3.2 mph

Although the angle to the actual wind has been changed 5°,
the apparent wind changes only 3°

Fig. 21

ally it may be due to the fact that the boat you happen to be watching has just gotten a nice puff, and it is generally better just to forget about it. However, if boats some distance off from you are definitely pointing higher all the time, this may mean that the wind is better over there and you had better go over and investigate; but *do not under any circumstances* attempt to point as high as you think the others are merely by heading your boat closer into the wind and pinching.

An experienced skipper can tell fairly well by the feel of his boat whether or not he is pointing it too high, except when the wind is practically nonexistent, but it is a good idea even for an experienced skipper to occasionally head the boat a little more into the wind and watch the jib and then bear off a little bit and just make sure that he was right. This feel is difficult to describe, as it is made up of many things, not all of them tangible. In medium and light winds, the angle of heel will lessen just as you start pointing too high; in a medium-to-high wind where the waves are not too high, the slapping of the waves against the hull will slow down as you point too high; in a very high wind there will generally be fairly big waves which will stop you noticeably if you are too high. In a very light wind where the wind won't even cause a piece of yarn to move, much less the sail, all that anyone can do is light a cigarette and steer by the smoke. Many skippers say they can sense the speed of the boat by the feel of the tiller. I have never been able to do this, as I never could detect any difference in the feel of the tiller until it was too late and I was already headed too high.

The most important thing to remember about going to windward is: You can't go along mentally picking daisies and beat the other boats to the windward mark. You must constantly be on the alert. This advice sounds trite, but it is amazing how many skippers could improve their scores by taking it to heart. Another good thing to remember is that most skippers point too high. It is difficult to tell just where the perfect point is, and it is a lot better to be a *little* too far off the wind than to be too close to it. Getting to the windward mark first is what counts—not trying to see who can outpoint whom.

On a reach the same principles apply concerning the trimming of sails— that is, let them out as far as possible without luffing. Most skippers trim their sails too flat on a reach. Generally it is not desirable to cleat the sheets when on a reach. The sails should be pulled in and the boat headed upwind as the wind drops; the sheets should be slacked off, and the boat should be headed out of the wind in gusts. In a medium light wind it is probably better just to hold a straight course, but to adjust the sheets for proper trim with variations of wind velocity. In very light winds it may pay to follow very much of a zig-zag course, bearing off fairly far with puffs in order to ride them as long as possible, then heading up quite far after the puff has passed in order to get the next one sooner. This doesn't always work, but it is worth a try.

Except in a light wind, the boom jack should always be rigged when on a reach or a run. It should be pulled quite tight so that the leech of the sail falls off as little as possible near the top. Rig it even in a light wind, if there are waves left over from a wind now gone or from power boats tearing around. (I know now why the cattlemen used to shoot the sheepherders and vice versa. It's a good thing that culture got to the West before sailboats did. The advent of water skiing makes one long for the good old days.)

There is much difference of opinion as to the point at which the jib should be poled out on the side opposite the main when on a broad reach. It is my opinion that this should be done as soon as the wind pennant points in a direction straight across the beam of the boat, except in very high winds where the pole will be hard to get out, or if it may be necessary to head upwind at any time in the near future. Setting the whisker pole at this point requires a long pole or the jib will not fill properly. I carry two whisker poles on my Snipe, one 90 inches long and one 86 inches—the longer one being preferred for broad reaching and the shorter one for a run. Either one can be used in either case if you happen to lose a pole in a high wind, which frequently happens. Most boats do not have whisker poles long enough to get the best efficiency out of the jib when set with the wind directly abeam. With a short pole, they have to let the pole go well forward before the jib will draw, giving a very inefficient shape to the jib.

Even with a long pole, it is not advisable to wing out when the apparent wind is much forward of directly across the boat. From this point forward it is better to take in the pole immediately. In trimming the jib with the pole out, just the opposite to the usual rule should be followed; the jib should be pulled back as far as possible instead of letting the sheet out as far as possible. In Figure 17 the apparent wind is too far forward to have the pole out, but Rosey wanted me to come closer to the boat he was on and I was too lazy to get the pole in.

The apparent wind direction at which the spinnaker may be hoisted on a reach is about the same as the point at which the jib should be poled out. The spinnaker can be carried in a very light wind with the apparent wind about a half point ahead of the beam, but as the wind velocity increases this point moves back until when the wind is at about the maximum at which you can handle the spinnaker, the apparent wind should be about a point behind the beam.

In putting either the whisker pole or spinnaker pole out, the crew should not go any farther forward than is absolutely necessary. In a light wind, his moving around will shake the sails, and in a high wind the boat is likely to broach if the crew gets very far forward on the deck. It is generally best for the skipper to handle the sheet until the crew has the pole set unless there are more than two people on the boat; and in very high winds when difficulty will be experienced in getting the pole out, the boat should be headed directly downwind, the pole should be pushed out straight ahead, and then the sail pulled back with the sheet after the pole has been set on the mast. Do not try to hold the sail back by bending the pole—all you will accomplish is breaking the pole. Just push on the pole, and trim with the sheet.

On a reach the jib fairlead should be farther out from the center line of the boat than on a beat. If your fairleads are well in from the sheer, you can use a snatch block on the sheer; in light winds the skipper or one of the crew can hold the sheet anywhere desired; but a pole cannot be used under either NAYRU or IYRU rules.

When reaching with a spinnaker, the sheet should be led as far aft and as far out as possible. The spinnaker pole should be trimmed so that it is at an angle of from 90 to 110 degrees to the apparent wind, depending on the boat, the length of the pole, and the cut of the spinnaker.

A good wind indicator is essential in order to tell when to set the spinnaker or whisker pole and to be able to tell on a run when you are about to jibe. About the most reliable, and certainly the cheapest, wind indicator is a piece of yarn tied to each stay. Yarn on the stays is not accurate on a run because of the flow of air around the mast off the main, but this can easily be allowed for. The yarn will indicate a jibe coming on before you are actually ready for a jibe. Generally, the yarn will make an angle of about ten degrees to the center line of the boat when the wind is dead astern. Some skippers try to use the wind pennant or yarn on a beat to tell whether they are pointing properly. I don't think this is at all efficient, at least on small boats, as the difference between pinching and not pinching is only a degree or so, and no wind indicator can give that accurate an indication. I look at the yarn on the stays frequently on a beat, particularly in a light shifty wind just to be sure that I haven't been absent-minded and headed way off below where I should be pointing, but that is the only use I make of it on a beat.

In a light wind which may turn into a drifting match, be sure to have lots of cigarettes and a lighter on board, as any kind of a wind indicator is worthless when little zephyrs of wind are coming from all directions when and if they come at all, and frequently these little zephyrs won't have any visible effect on the sails. Under these circumstances, there is nothing to sail by except the smoke from the cigarette.

2. Handling the Boat

THE MOST IMPORTANT THING ABOUT HANDLING THE BOAT IS TO HOLD IT AS flat as possible. This of course does not apply to the inland-lake scow, or similar boats which are designed to sail on their ear, but with any other type of small boat you won't go anywhere if you let the boat heel.

It may be lots of fun to sail around with your lee rail under, but your smarter racing competitors will be very happy to see you do so. The boat should never be allowed to heel more than 10 or 15 degrees, *even momentarily*. In a very light wind it is helpful to force the boat to heel about this much by sitting on the low side; this will enable gravity to help what little wind there is to fill the sails properly. At all other times, hold the boat as flat as possible. In very high winds this will be made much easier by using flat sails and by carrying the boom down as low as possible without causing too much inconvenience in moving about in the boat.

The chief means, however, of holding a small sailboat flat is for the skipper and crew to get out as far as possible in order to balance the boat. This does not mean just sitting on the edge of the boat. The skipper and the crew should be provided with straps or some other device to hook their feet under in order to enable them to really get out. This, of course, is a little hard on the stomach muscles, but it is really astonishing how much faster a boat will move when the skipper and crew lean out so that their legs are straight, their bodies are horizontal, and they are entirely outside of the boat except from their feet up to slightly above their knees. The length of the extension on the tiller should be such that the skipper can get out this way and allow the tiller to remain near the center of the boat, which is where it will be if the boat is rigged properly and it is not allowed to heel. With the use of two hiking straps as shown in Figure 9 I found that I could get out enough farther and stay there long enough that I had to change the length of the tiller extension from 18 inches to 24 inches.

Many skippers and crews seem to think that by merely draping themselves along or over the sheer, they are doing a high-class job of balancing the boat. This seems to be particularly popular on Stars that are being photographed. Maybe it is a result of a mistaken desire to reduce air resistance—but in any case, it is mistaken. The important thing in a high wind is to hold the boat flat—the increased drive of the boat will more than compensate for the air resistance of the upper halves of a couple of bodies projecting horizontally from the sheer. The center of gravity of the human form moves about $16\frac{1}{2}$ inches farther out when horizontal, and perpendicular to the boat center line, than when draped along the sheer. The silliest thing to do is to lie on one's tummy in order to hang onto the tiller and try to balance the boat by holding the feet out. In this case, the center of gravity is about 20 inches farther in than it should be. (I have learned that there is apparently a rule against hiking straps in the Star class; however, some of the skippers have started leaning out, using a secret weapon that looks suspiciously like a tiller extension. The whole procedure is however shrouded in secrecy and very little information is available for publication.)

A rather spectacular and very effective way of balancing the boat is for the crew to stand on the sheer, leaning out from this point by hanging onto a line tied either to the mast or to the stays. If you use stays with swaged fittings, before the lower fitting is swaged onto your side stays slide on a stainless steel or brass washer about $\frac{1}{2}$-inch diameter and one of the standard stainless steel ball fittings. Swage this ball onto the stay about three feet above the lower end. You can then tie a rope around the stay, and the washer and ball will prevent its sliding down the stay. If your class prohibits use of "trapeze rigs" this is probably illegal, but there is nothing against just grabbing the stay which is actually quite easy.

Many people think that this will increase the load in the stay and mast. It may, but not for the reason they think. Pulling the stay out of a straight line, assuming the leeward stay is slack, will actually decrease the tension on the stay and the compression in the mast. The angle between the stay and the mast becomes greater, which of course causes the loads to be less. However, balancing the boat this way permits the crew to hold the boat up with more wind and therefore more heeling tendency—so the load in the mast and stay remains about the same.

This method can be used only with fairly steady winds and requires a young and agile crew. Also, the lines that he uses to hang onto occasionally get tangled in the jib sheet, but if the crew has had enough practice at it and is very sure-footed, it is a very effective means of holding the boat down when this cannot be done by merely leaning out of the boat.

In the sketch, Figure 22, an equation is set up for the lateral and vertical forces acting on a 450-pound sailboat when it is heeling at a 15-degree angle to illustrate the value of really getting out to balance a small boat. Five different positions are shown for the center-of-gravity locations of skippers and crews balancing the boat by various means. The respective locations, the moment arms, and the amount of heeling tendency that can be balanced by a 150-pound skipper and a 150-pound crew (5 feet, 10 inches tall) are as follows:

In Position 1, the skipper and crew are leaning out, but with their feet braced against the opposite side of the cockpit. Their moment arm is 28 inches and the value of H is therefore:

$$28(1.22) + 28(1.22) + 30 = 98.5 \text{ lbs.}$$

The moment arm of a skipper and crew lying on their stomachs with their feet hanging over the sheer is the same as Position 1.

In Position 2, the skipper and crew are draped along the sheer and are well streamlined—if they can hold the boat down with their moment arm which is 33 inches, which will balance a heeling force of 110.8 pounds, 13 percent more than with the skipper and crew in Position 1.

In Position 3, the skipper and crew are doing what most people consider a good job of balancing a boat—but their legs are not straight, and their bodies are at about a 45-degree angle instead of horizontal. Their moment arm is 40.5 inches, and the heeling force they can balance is 129 pounds, 31 percent more than with the skipper and crew in Position 1, and 16 percent more than in Position 2.

In Position 4, both the skipper and crew are doing an excellent job of getting out—their legs are straight and their bodies are horizontal. Their moment arm is 49.5 inches, and the heeling force which they can balance is 151 pounds, almost 54 percent more than in Position 1, and 17 percent more than in Position 3 which most people think is pretty good.

Position 5 is the center of gravity of a crew standing on the sheer, hanging onto a line attached to the stay, leaning out at a 45-degree angle. The heeling tendency which can be balanced by the crew in this position, with the skipper in Position 4 is 168.5 pounds, 72 percent more than Position 1 and 12 percent better than with both at Position 4.

Figure 23 shows Ernie Coleman and his crew doing the best job of holding down a Snipe on a beat that I have ever seen photographed. At the moment the picture was snapped, they are not leaning out as far as they can because the wind has apparently dropped momentarily; however, they are

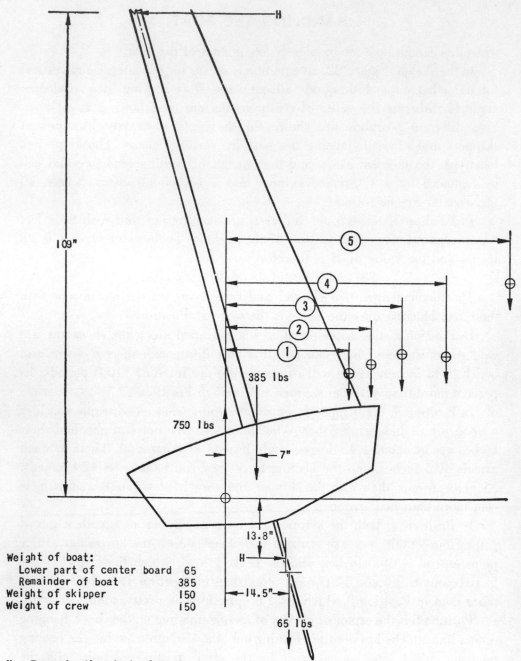

109"

⑤

④

③

②

①

385 lbs

750 lbs

7"

13.8"

H

14.5"

65 lbs

Weight of boat:
  Lower part of center board 65
  Remainder of boat 385
Weight of skipper 150
Weight of crew 150

H = Force tending to heel boat
    (resisted by equal force at center of lateral resistance)
X = Moment arm to center of gravity of skipper
Y = Moment arm to center of gravity of crew

Basic equation for equilibrium: ΣM_O: $H = \dfrac{150X + 150Y + (385 \times 7) + (65 \times 14.5)}{(109 + 13.8)}$

$$H = 1.22X + 1.22Y + 30$$

Fig. 22

58

completely out of the boat except for their legs from slightly above the knees, and when a gust comes they can immediately lean out farther and keep the boat from heeling any more. The angle of heel to which they are holding the boat is about as close to vertical as is practical.

To illustrate the relative importance of the skipper and crew as compared with the centerboard in balancing the boat, a 150-pound skipper and crew moving their center of gravity one-half inch farther out on a Snipe is equivalent to increasing the weight of the centerboard from 62 to 80 pounds when the boat is held to a 15-degree angle of heel. The flatter the boat is held, the less the centerboard counts.

Holding the boat flat is just as important on a reach as on a beat, especially when there is enough wind for the boat to plane. Some boats even go better heeled to windward on a reach in a medium wind. The fore-and-aft balance of the boat should be slightly forward of that on a beat, particularly in very light winds.

With heavier and larger boats, the crew weight becomes a smaller percentage of the total and the effect on balance of the skipper and crew getting out becomes less. The effect will still be appreciable, however, until you get to a fairly large boat, and it may be just enough to make the difference between winning and not winning in a close race.

There is no such thing as an absolutely steady wind, either as far as direction or velocity is concerned. This means that if the boat is being balanced for the average wind, it will tend to heel over in the gusts. If the wind is not too high, the boat can be balanced by the skipper and crew getting out farther in the gust and crawling back as the gust passes. If they are already out as far as they can go balancing the wind before the gust, something else must be done. On a reach, slack off the main and bear off in the gust. Head back up and pull in the main when the gust passes.

When beating to windward and the skipper and crew are out as far as they can get balancing the average wind, the thing to do in the gust is to head the boat into the wind slightly, letting the jib luff until the gust is past. It takes a lot of practice to head the boat into the wind soon enough to prevent any additional heeling over and then to head it back out of the wind again at the right moment to prevent the boat heeling to windward, but the boat can be kept at a constant angle of heel through a gust without the crew moving.

If the waves are not too high, the gust may be seen coming on the surface of the water; however, with high waves the gust must be felt and the tiller pushed down immediately. It is for this reason that a wood extension on the tiller is better than rope, as the boat must sometimes be luffed very sharply to prevent heeling. Luffing through gusts is an astonishingly effective way of keeping the boat going and working to windward at the same time. I have watched two boats sailing close together running into the same gust; the boat which luffs into the puff will gain about ten feet in forward distance and about three or four feet in progress to windward over the other boat which is merely allowed to heel with the gust. If the other skipper slacks off his main also to stop the heeling, the boat which has luffed into the gust will gain as much as 20 feet.

I have worked out of a hopeless position immediately behind another boat and worked past him to windward or to leeward on about three gusts when the other boat was allowed to heel. I have also been taken by another boat on a couple of gusts when I wasn't sharp enough to luff immediately and the other skipper was. This advice may seem to be contrary to the earlier advice to not point quite as high in high waves, as high winds are normally accompanied by waves; however, the luffing recommended here is only in gusts and the boat should be immediately headed off the wind to its best sailing point as soon as it is possible for the skipper and crew to hold the boat flat.

It took only about one minute to read the preceding paragraphs, but it will take a year or two to be able to work out the technique that I am talking about. It took me eight years, but nobody told me what to do in words of one syllable that sunk in—I finally figured it out by watching John Hayward beat me every time the wind blew hard. John had written an article a year or so before in "Jib Sheet" on the subject of reducing weather helm by luffing, but it didn't sink in.

I also have a suspicion that many skippers will say that maybe it works on a Snipe but it won't work on their boats. This is another case where Mr. Kettering was right—they know it won't work because that just isn't the way to sail in high winds. I have done it in a Hagerty Sea Shell, and I have seen it done—very rarely, but successfully—on Sea Gulls, and a friend of mine who sails on the Pacific tells me it works on his 46-foot yawl, so I don't think the technique can be limited to Snipes. Dr. Curry recommends it for large boats, but his recommended technique for small boats is entirely different. I hope all my rivals believe Curry and not me. Unfortunately, the majority of my competitors now seem to have adopted the system.

Maybe the reason it took me so long is that in Kansas the gusts come quicker, blow harder, and quit more suddenly than any place else that I have ever sailed. The wind also has a nasty habit of shifting very suddenly

about 15 degrees every now and then when it is blowing hard, with the result
that in Wichita you are more apt to capsize to windward than to leeward in
a high wind, and a skipper has a pardonable tendency to pay more attention
to staying right side up than he does to learning the finer points of luffing
through gusts. Any place else, the technique should be a lot easier to perfect.

A good way to practice is to go out when the wind is not too high and
practice holding the boat to a constant angle of heel by using the tiller without the skipper or crew moving. Another good way to practice this, without
involving too much effort, is to go in a high wind without the jib and try
the same thing. Leaving off the jib will let you practice longer before you are
worn out.

If you are going to win races in high winds, this technique must be
developed. You have to learn to practically smell the gust coming and start
to luff before it gets there and to start to bear off before it leaves. Keep
your mainsheet cleated all the time. *Do not*, except as a last resort, let out
your main.

Sailing with the main cleated in a high wind is a big help to the skipper
when coming about, as he pays no attention to the mainsheet and concentrates
on balancing the boat and getting it headed on its new course. Leaving the
main cleated in a high wind will scare the skipper badly at first, but when
he has developed the technique of luffing into the gusts he will be astonished
at how seldom it is necessary to ever uncleat the main on a beat. Probably
the biggest advantage, however, is that keeping the main cleated in a high
wind will *force* the skipper to learn to luff through the puffs and therefore
to sail his boat most efficiently. This technique is of course most effective
with flat sails, but can be used when you are caught with sails that are too
full by just not trimming the main in so far. The cleat should, of course, be
arranged so that it can be released immediately, and the skipper should
always hold the sheet in case it should be necessary to release it when sailing
in high winds. After a considerable amount of practice, it is possible to sail
in winds up to 35 miles an hour without ever uncleating the main on a beat
even in the gusty winds experienced in the Midwest. In addition to not
having to bother about the mainsheet when coming about, cleating of the
main allows the skipper to devote his attention to handling the boat, watching
others, and in a high wind allows him to save his energy for balancing the
boat instead of fighting the mainsheet.

Some day there is going to be a good argument when a boat being sailed
fast in a high wind overtakes to leeward a boat which is being allowed to
heel and is therefore not going as fast. Although theoretically it is impossible

in the case of two evenly-matched boats for one to sail through the lee of the other on a beat and close enough to the windward boat so that they might touch each other, it can easily be done in a strong gusty wind if the leeward boat is sailing properly and the windward one is being allowed to heel way over—particularly if the windward one has been caught with full sails. The same situation could arise in a race with different classes of boats when a faster, closer-winded boat was overtaking a slower one which couldn't point as high, although there would probably be a little less argument in the latter case.

From a careful reading of the rules and the definitions it would seem that B in Figure 24 has the right of way and that A had better tack and get out of there, providing B left A ample room and opportunity to keep clear when he established an overlap. It is a good idea for B to hail also, although it is not required.

On most small boats the fore-and-aft location of the skipper and the crew should be approximately in the center of the boat, sitting a little farther forward in light winds with no waves and a little farther back with higher winds and high waves. Also, the weight should generally be carried farther forward on a reach and a run than on a beat. On a Snipe with the cockpit at the forward limit, this means having the crew on the deck just in front of the cockpit in a very light wind, just at the front of the cockpit in a medium wind, and about six or eight inches farther back in a high wind.

In light winds the most important thing is to sit still and not jump around in the boat. When it is necessary to move, move slowly so as not to shake out what little wind there is in the sails. When it is not necessary to get out to balance the boat, the crew should lie down on the deck or sit in the bottom of the boat. It may seem silly to worry about such a small thing as air resistance on the skipper and crew in a light wind; however, many times the difference between first and second place in a race will be one second in a race lasting several hours. In this case the person losing the race would have only had to improve his speed by a factor of 1.0001 in order to win. This may also sound contradictory to my remarks made earlier about trying to save wind resistance in a high wind by draping yourself over the sheer. It isn't—it is merely a question of deciding which is most important under the existing conditions. In a high wind, it is most important to balance the boat. In lighter winds this can be done easily, so it is most important to cut down wind resistance.

A couple of seconds would have done a lot of good for two boats in the photograph, Figure 25, which was taken with a telephoto lens from the

FIG. 23

Ernie Coleman and Jed Hanna demonstrating how a small sailboat should be sailed in a strong wind.

FIG. 25

The finish line is actually almost parallel to the bottom of the picture —the skippers of 4193, 6911, and 9 (hidden behind 4193) would have given a lot for a couple of seconds here.

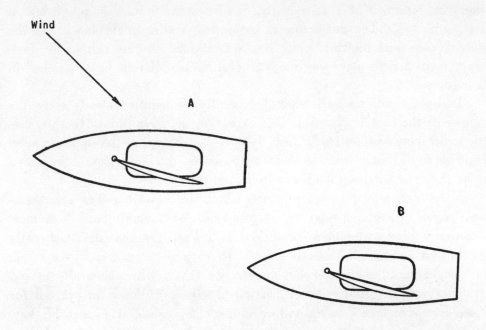

Wind

A

B

Fig. 24

Both yachts are close-hauled; however, A is unable to point as high or go as fast as B (for example, because it is shortly after the start and A had been killing time, or the wind is high and the skipper of A lets his boat heel too much). When Yacht B establishes her overlap, she must give Yacht A sufficient room to luff sharply or tack without her stern swinging into B. From this time on, however, A must keep clear if Yacht B is sailing no higher than her normal course. (See definition -- in this case, close-hauled or in a high wind, luffing enough to balance the boat.) If A falls off on B, she must not touch B as B is the leeward boat and has right-of-way. After the overlap is established, B is no longer the overtaking yacht and becomes the right-of-way yacht. Her only obligations are to give A room to maneuver when establishing the overlap and thereafter to sail no higher than her normal course.

shore at the finish of a race in the Southwestern Snipe Championship in Dallas in 1949. The finish line is not quite parallel to the bottom of the photograph—and the third-place boat was about four feet behind the first-place boat. Fourth place was about 20 feet back—all four boats finished in five seconds.

In light winds the sails should generally be handled slowly when the course of the boat is changed. One exception is when jibing. In this case the main should be pulled in fast, then let out slowly on the opposite side. Hauling in the boom with the sheets is too slow—the boom should be pulled in by the crew handling the boom itself, not the sheets.

Very high waves, especially those which are close together and therefore steep, create a special set of problems for a small boat. The most important thing under these conditions is to keep the boat dry. Generally the largest waves will come in groups. There will be several waves which are larger than the average, but these large waves do not generally extend over very much distance. When beating to windward, keep an eye out for these groups of larger waves and avoid them if possible. This may be done by luffing up to let them go past or bearing off and getting by them before they get to you. When you cannot miss them, the proper technique is to bear off just a little just before the top of the wave. If the next wave is not too close you can head up again, even to the point of luffing slightly, as you coast down the wave—then bear off just before the top of the next wave. If the waves are too close together to do this, as they will be in shallow water, you can at least do it on every other wave. Just go ahead and crash through the intervening ones. When the waves are breaking, bearing off is dangerous as the boat may be filled with water by a single wave, or it may just simply be knocked over by the force of the wave. In this case, it is better to luff up and head as nearly as possible into the wave. You will still take on plenty of water, but there is less chance of being swamped or capsized.

In a high wind (35 miles an hour or so) on a very close reach, it will sometimes be necessary to slack off the main slightly in order to cut down the forward drive of the sails tending to nose the bow under even though you can balance the boat with the sails trimmed in. It is possible under these conditions with the sails trimmed for the best speed to drive the boat so hard that the bow will not rise over the crest of the waves, and a great deal of water will be taken on even though the waves are not too high. In these circumstances it is better to slack off the main a little bit until the bow rides over the waves better. Moving the skipper and the crew aft to try to prevent this is not very effective, as the drive of the sails is so much greater than the effect of a small movement of the skipper-and-crew weight. This happens only on rare occasions, but it does happen.

Always remember in bad waves that it is more important to keep the boat dry than to get the maximum theoretical speed from the boat. A boat with very much water in it just simply will not go. Also, when going before a wind, a boat with very much water in it will become completely unmanageable in high waves, particularly if they are close together and steep. The boat should be kept as dry as possible on the beat, first by taking in as little water as possible, by dodging the big waves or bearing off on the others as mentioned above, by having spray boards which are really worth something, and by bailing while on the beat either with a rope attached to a good built-in pump or by a long bilge pump with which the crew can reach the low side of the boat while leaning out to balance the boat. However, if in spite of all this the boat still has a lot of water in it at the time you reach the windward mark, do not plan on bailing on the downwind leg as you will probably be swimming instead of bailing very shortly after rounding the mark. The best thing to do under these circumstances is to luff the boat into the wind and bail it fairly dry before rounding the mark. This seems like a poor way to win races, but I spent an hour and a half hanging onto a submerged boat in the Gulf of Mexico one December because I didn't do it. The boat didn't capsize—it just spun in off the top of a wave about one hundred feet after rounding the windward mark. Of course, a small boat has no business racing under these conditions, but they do it sometimes.

When beating to windward in big waves, make up your mind about tacking as far ahead of time as possible. There will be patches where the waves are smaller just like there are patches where they are larger than average, and the boat should be brought about in these patches where possible. In any case, do not hit a wave just as the boat heads into the wind, as the boat is very likely to stop and go in stays. Going into stays in a high wind with big waves is a hazardous and very unprofitable occupation. Even if you want to tack for the mark, and will overstand the mark if you keep going, it is still better to do so—no matter how quickly you can right a capsized boat.

What to do when you get caught in a squall or thunderstorm depends of course on how bad the storm is going to be. The problem is to tell this before it is too late. In the Midwest, when you see a big black cloud and lightning, you can expect the worst. If the race committee is smart, they will call off the race before the storm gets too close. If they don't, as soon as the wind shifts and starts to come out of the storm, head into the wind, drop your sails, and get the anchor out. In the Midwest, discretion is definitely the better part of valor in a thunderstorm, as winds over 70 miles an hour are customary. I tried sailing through one going to windward on the jib after dropping the main once and broke a mast in the process. I tried sailing through another one because it came up in the course of a race in the Midwestern Snipe Championship. The weather bureau reported the wind at 75 miles an hour afterward. The boat I had at that time had a cockpit only 18 inches wide, and while strictly speaking we didn't capsize, our method of getting to shore was somewhat unorthodox. My crew was standing on the centerboard holding the jib sheet while I was in the water holding onto the rudder. The top of the mast would get three or four feet above the water before getting slapped down again, but we got to shore without any water in the boat. I don't recommend this procedure, however. The only reason it worked here was that the storm came up suddenly on a small lake and the waves did not have time to build up, and also we were not far from shore. Those hailstones bouncing off your head don't feel good.

Along the coast, the storms are not normally so severe (the exception of course being the one off Larchmont on the Fourth of July, 1949), and it is generally possible to sail through them. The safest place to be when a storm hits is heading into it on a beat. On a reach you are apt to be blown over even with all sails free if the wind is over 50 miles an hour; and on a run you may easily lose your mast, particularly if you don't have a permanent back stay. If the wind stays over about 45 miles an hour for any length of time, you will do better by dropping the jib. It is surprising how well a normally sloop-rigged boat will handle in a squall under the main alone, particularly if you have been fighting it with a good-sized genoa up.

If the wind has been blowing fairly hard up to the time the squall hits (which it generally doesn't in the case of a thunderstorm) a run may be the safest place to be caught by the storm, as the boat will be moving fast and the impact of the blow may then not be hard enough to dismast you. The chief disadvantage of a run is that it will be difficult, if not impossible, to head up to a beat without capsizing if you run out of water before the squall lets up, and it is likely to be difficult to drop your sails on a run without damage to your main.

In any case—if you see a storm coming, drop your boom as low as you can while you still have a chance, reef if you can, and put on your life preservers. And if you are really smart, you will consider safety first, and the possibility of winning the race, if there is still a race, secondary.

When coming about, the crew should always release the jib the instant that it starts to shake (do not hold it until it is backwinded), and in high winds the skipper and crew should get to the high side, lean all the way out, and trim the sails all at the same time. No attempt should be made by the crew to get the jib sheet into the jam cleat (unless it can be popped in with neither time nor effort as is the case in the arrangement shown in Figure 8) or wrapped around a winch while coming about, as too much time will be lost. Get the boat on its way, then luff up into the wind and cleat down the jib sheet. This whole procedure is not easy to accomplish in high winds, but it is of vital importance.

Some skippers recommend bearing off slightly to get the boat started after tacking. This is necessary if you have allowed the boat to stop by turning on either too small or too large a radius, but with a small boat it shouldn't be necessary. It is particularly bad in a high wind as it will be necessary to slack off on the sheets to keep from heeling too much when bearing off, and it will be difficult to get them trimmed in again. Remember —get over fast, get way out, and trim the jib in flat. The important thing is to hold the boat down flat and get it moving on its new tack immediately after it is in a position where the sails will fill. If you do all of this fast enough, you won't need to bear off to get the boat moving again.

If a stop is rigged to limit the rudder travel, the skipper can merely let go of the tiller when he wants to come about and pick it up when he gets to the opposite side. In a light wind, the tiller should be given a good shove before releasing it, and with no wind it may be necessary to pump it quite a bit to get the boat around. While sculling is of course illegal, assisting the boat to come about when there isn't any wind has been allowed providing the tiller is not moved beyond the centerline of the boat in the process.

When jibing, never turn loose of the tiller as it will be on the wrong side of the cockpit when you have finished your jibe, and it may be hard to get hold of it soon enough. Also, your jibe is likely to be much too fast with the tiller free. In a high wind always uncleat the mainsheet and hold it in your hand while jibing. Nothing will capsize you faster than having the mainsheet get snarled up when jibing in a high wind.

Many skippers consider jibing in a high wind to be hazardous and prefer to come about even if it means overshooting a mark. While a jibe in a high wind is admittedly a pretty wild maneuver, I feel that in a small boat properly rigged there is less chance of capsizing in a well-done jibe in a very high wind than there is by being caught by a puff just as you are finished coming about and before you have regained your forward speed.

If you are planing when you want to jibe, try to stop by bearing off unless you are already dead before the wind, and by moving back as far as possible. If you will be on a run on the opposite tack after jibing, set the whisker pole and the jib in front of the main before you jibe. This will help slow you down if you are planing, and it is much easier to get the pole set with the main shielding the jib. If you will be on a beat or a reach after jibing, just let the jib flap for enough time before jibing to stop planing. If you can't stop planing in spite of your efforts, go ahead and jibe but be sure you don't get tangled up in anything.

The safest jibe in a high wind is made by bearing off until you are a little beyond directly before the wind, trimming the main in slowly until it flops over. As soon as the main goes over, bear off immediately and sharply on the new course to avoid being headed suddenly up into the wind. The main should be let run very freely until it is as far out as it can go (Figure 26).

For obvious reasons the centerboard should be all the way down when making this maneuver, although the boom jack should be left on (if it is rigged to the center of the boat). The skipper and crew should be on their toes ready to hike out on the high side when the jibe is completed, and the crew can also help by assisting the boom to come over when it is just about ready to.

In a high wind, most small boats will climb up out of the water and plane like a speed boat on a broad reach or a run. Minimum weight and smooth, well-sharpened under-water surfaces are particularly important in getting the boat to start planing as soon as possible and in keeping it up there as long as possible. Keeping the boat flat is also essential. With small waves such as are found on inland lakes even with high winds, not very much can be done to make the boat plane when it is on the verge of it or to keep it planing when it wants to stop, except to be very careful of the trim of the sails when reaching; however, on big waves on either a run or a very broad reach, the boat will plane on the top of the waves like a surf board, and planing can be started earlier and continued longer by "ooching." I'm not sure of the origin of either the word or of the process, and as far as using means other than sails for propulsion goes, ooching is as effective as starting the engine, but it has not been ruled illegal as of this moment. Another system is to rapidly pull in the main and let it out, but I don't think this is nearly as effective as ooching. I have recently seen what looked like a performance by a couple of people in the last throes of St. Vitus dance, the skipper and crew bouncing up and down on the deck any time it looked like the boat ought to plane. I think this has more effect on the mental outlook of those doing it than it does on the boat.

The ooching process consists of the crew standing in a crouching position and taking a firm hold of the boat—either the mast and the sheer, the top

Start to bear off, put out whisker
pole on same side as main, and cleat
the jib sheet so the pole won't fall
down. Continue to bear off while
pulling in on main. When the boom is
almost ready to go over, crew should
help it.

Wind

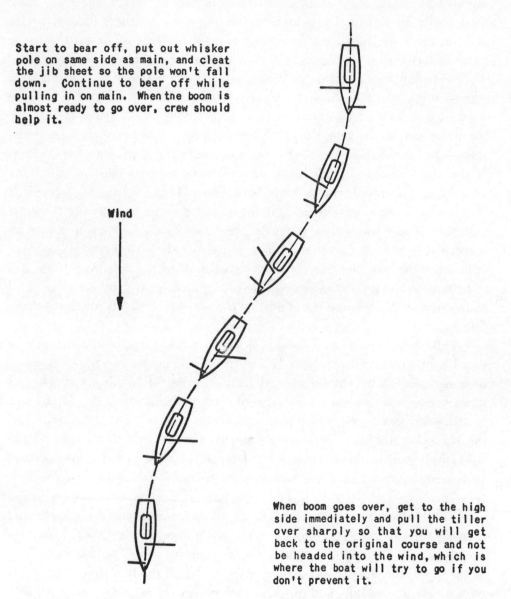

When boom goes over, get to the high
side immediately and pull the tiller
over sharply so that you will get
back to the original course and not
be headed into the wind, which is
where the boat will try to go if you
don't prevent it.

Fig. 26

69

of the centerboard trunk and the edge of the cockpit, or anything else that is firmly tied on—and then trying to shake the boat to pieces. The shaking consists of a series of violent forward lunges at a frequency of about 50 a minute. The lunges must not be half-hearted to be really effective—they must really be violent. The skipper in the meantime balances the boat, tries to keep the boat from broaching or generally heading off toward Jones's, hangs onto the edge of the cockpit, and ooches in unison with the crew.

The technique is to start ooching just as the bow drops as a result of a wave coming up under the stern. Unless you are running directly before the wind, it is a good idea to bear off so as to be more nearly perpendicular to the wave just as the bow drops. When ooching is properly done, and the waves are high enough the boat seems to practically jump out of the water. If the wind velocity or the height of the wave is somewhat marginal for planing, the boat will tend to settle back down if the ooching is stopped. It is therefore continued either until the planing stops anyway or the crew collapses. There was a time when the crew could look forward to a rest on a reach or a run after a tough beat in a high wind; however, when ooching is in order the beat becomes the most restful part of the race, as all that has to be done is to stay stationary outside of the boat from your knees up, bail constantly, and occasionally climb back in a hurry to keep from getting dunked.

While I have only seen ooching done on Snipes, it should work on any small boat which will plane fairly readily. If the boat won't plane anyway, ooching won't help. On larger and heavier types of planing sailboats, its effectiveness will depend on the ratio of crew weight to boat weight. I know it will work on a Snipe, which planes easily in spite of what Bob Bavier, Jr. thinks, where the total crew weight is about two-thirds the weight of the boat empty—with a lower ratio of live to dead weight it will of course become less effective. Don't give up, however, if it doesn't work the first time—it takes practice and perfect unison on the part of the oochers.

With really high waves, all rules are off as far as where the skipper and crew should sit when reaching or running. Planing on waves will generally start better by having the weight fairly far forward. This is all right as long as the top of the stem is still above the water, but if the bow dives under, get back as far as possible, and quickly. This maneuver generally ends up with the skipper sitting on the transom with the tiller over his head and the crew on his lap. For some reason, wiggling the tiller rapidly back and forth seems to help unsubmerge. Another time when discretion is the better part of valor is when planing on the crest of waves which are close together and really high. In this case the entire front half of the boat will be out of the water hanging over the trough in front of the wave, and the skipper and crew had better be sitting on the transom. Due to the fact that the water right at the crest of the wave is moving faster than the wave when the wave is on the verge of breaking, the boat will sometimes practically take off and fly when the wave on which it is planing decides to break. It scoots up onto the next wave ahead and starts planing there. This is fine if the boat doesn't do a flip flop in the process. Under these conditions the skipper and crew must be ready to jump in any direction quickly, as the boat would just as soon capsize into the wind as with the wind, and frequently seems to have a suppressed desire to become a submarine. Under these conditions, illogical as it may sound at first, the centerboard should be up instead of down. The reason for this is that if the boat gets hit even slightly broadside by the breaking wave it will flit with the board down. If the board is up, it merely slides sideways and you have a chance of getting it aimed in the right direction again before it swaps ends.

Again the most important thing is to keep the boat dry; even a fairly small amount of water sloshing around in the bottom will make it unmanageable. If you know that these conditions will exist before the start of a race, put on high spray boards which come all the way out to the sheer of the boat. Mae Wests are not a bad idea, either. Put them on—their weight will help you balance the boat if you are wearing them, and they do not do any good stowed away in the boat. Also, as I have found from sad experience, they are hard to find and harder to put on after you have capsized.

On a broad reach with a centerboard boat, do not yield to the temptation to pull the centerboard up too far. A well-sharpened board will have very little drag, and if the board is pulled up too high on a reach, the tendency of the boat to drift sideways will cause the board to be working at a very high angle of attack, and the drag will be increased over what it would have been with the board down a little farther. Also, on a run always leave enough of the board down in the water to keep the slot in the keel closed up. Pulling the board all the way up so that water can flow into this slot will increase the drag instead of reducing it if your board is smooth and well sharpened. If it is rough and has square edges, pull it up. Pivot boards will sometimes jam if an attempt is made to lower them while on a reach in a good wind. Heading directly downwind and shaking the boat a little will generally free them. (Remember this if you are a dagger board man and are sailing a borrowed pivot board boat in a race.)

Develop a standard routine for each maneuver, such as when rounding a mark onto a run. Always put the pole out first, put on the boom jack next, and raise the centerboard last; (better yet—put on the boom jack before you round the mark if it is rigged to the boat centerline). In developing these standard routines, remember to do things in the order of their importance as far as making the boat go fast. In the example just given, the sequence is very important. The poling out of the jib or setting the spinnaker has much more effect on the speed of the boat than anything else. The boom jack is next, and the centerboard is least important.

A standard procedure can be worked out for other things also, such as jibing on a run, rounding marks, etc. Practice these so that you and the crew know what each of you is going to do and when. No matter how much you race, practicing this way is a good idea throughout the season—you just simply cannot be good without practicing—no matter how smart you are. In close competition you may frequently have to act quickly, and you won't have time to tell your crew what to do. In these cases, practice will prevent bungling up a maneuver.

After you have followed all of the suggestions that have been given above on how to get the most out of your boat and your sails, there is still one more thing to learn, and this will be the most difficult—that is to avoid the nautical equivalent of "buck fever." Many good skippers with good boats, when just playing around can keep up with the best, but they never succeed in placing high in official point-score races. Others who do very well in their own club point-score races will not do nearly as well as they should in big regattas. Curing this disease is very difficult. Probably the best cure is to have enough practice in sailing so that you have confidence in yourself and your equipment; then try to remain calm and take it easy while racing. I do not mean to suggest taking it easy to the extent of sailing a sloppy race, but I do recommend taking it easy to the extent of not worrying to the point where you start pressing too hard. There are times when this is easier said than done.

The best way to demonstrate the existence of this nautical equivalent of buck fever is to have a handicap race in which all of the boats are started at different times, their starts being timed so that theoretically they will all finish at the same time. The amount of time they are given on the start is determined from their previous performance in official races. The skippers who are really good but who fold up under pressure will generally finish far ahead of the time at which they should finish in the case of a handicap race with no one pressing them. A few races such as this are helpful in building up the morale of the less successful skippers—it shows them that if they would only relax, they would do a lot better.

PART III

Racing Tactics

I. General Principles of Starting

ONE OF THE BEST WAYS TO LOSE RACES IS TO LEAVE THE DOCK AT THE LAST minute and dash madly for the starting line, arriving a minute or so before the start. Under these conditions you generally arrive in a somewhat flustered condition and have no opportunity to get the feel of the boat under the conditions in which you will be racing, and you have no opportunity for last-minute adjustments on the sails. The best thing to do is to go out about an hour or an hour and a half before the race and sail around for awhile to be sure that everything is working properly. This gives a final check on whether you have forgotten anything, and you can also at this time check the sails that you are planning to use, doing as good a job as possible at guessing what the wind is going to be at the actual race time.

It is very desirable to have a wind velocity estimator, although the location at which you are checking the wind is frequently somewhat sheltered, and a certain amount of guesswork will be involved as to what the wind velocity is where you are going to race; and of course the wind usually changes after you get to the starting line. However, a wind velocity estimator will improve your guessing average greatly.

When in doubt, use a medium draft mainsail which is of full dimensions. This sail will be far superior to a full sail in a wind over about 15 to 20 miles an hour and not too inferior down to about 5 to 10 miles an hour. It is also far superior to a flat sail in a wind of 20 miles an hour, not bad at around 25 miles an hour, and not too much inferior in winds around 30 miles an hour. A heavy skipper and crew can increase these velocities some, and lighter ones should decrease them some. The principle is: If you are *sure* the wind will not be too much for full sails, use them; if in doubt, use medium draft ones, full size. If you are *sure* the wind is too much for medium cut sails, use flat ones; if in doubt, use the medium ones. Incidentally, there is no more hopeless situation than trying to race in a light wind with small flat sails. As a matter of fact, you can quite satisfactorily take care of all conditions in which you have any business racing with one suit of sails—medium draft, full size. The flat main is valuable only if you are racing in a wind where it amounts to an endurance contest instead of a race, or if you and your crew are both quite light.

During hot weather along the coast the breeze over the water is likely to be much stronger during the hottest part of the day than it is over the land, and you will get badly fooled by calling the local airport for wind velocity. The wind along the shore near a large body of water in hot weather is made up of the normal surface wind, which is in the same direction but at a lower velocity than the upper-air wind, and the sea breeze which is caused by the air mass over the land being heated more than the air mass over the sea. The air mass over the land tends to rise, pulling in air from over the sea. This sea breeze apparently dissipates rapidly when it reaches the land, and when there is a strong on-shore breeze on a hot afternoon the wind velocity on the water may be as much as 10 or 15 miles an hour higher than the wind velocity given at an airport several miles inland. On inland lakes you can get fooled equally well in the other direction—the wind velocity on top of a control tower 75 feet above the ground at the airport may be lots more than the wind down on the water, particularly if the lake is surrounded by hills or trees. And regardless of where you are, it doesn't do any good to know what the wind is blowing 15 or 20 miles away at an airport unless of course there is a front coming. I have seen La Guardia airport give 20 to 30 miles an hour and yet Larchmont remained a dead calm.

After your preliminary sailing around, and after guessing what the wind will be, you should get to the starting line ready to race at least 30 minutes before the start. Whenever the starting line is a long way from the mooring, it is a good idea to carry a spare mainsail with you. The wind may have either come up or dropped after leaving the mooring, and it takes very little time to either anchor or tie up behind a spectator boat and change the main if you should need to. Don't wait until the last second to make up your mind, however—something is bound to go haywire if you try to change sails in a frantic scramble. You can usually dump the spare sail on the committee boat or a spectator boat so that you don't have to carry it around, but even if you can't get rid of it, its weight won't hurt you enough to worry about.

It is best to carry two stop watches, not only in case something happens to one of them but also so that you can take the time remaining yourself when you cross the line in the reverse direction and decide when you wish to come about for the actual start. The crew should also have a watch so that he can start counting seconds about five seconds before you want to come about and to give you the time remaining until the gun goes off while you are heading for the line.

No matter how much experience you have in timing starts, remember to watch the flags. Check your time on each flag and gun, and particularly if you do not hear the starting gun, look for the flag signals on the committee boat. Arguing with a race committee is like arguing with a traffic cop—they are never wrong. And in the end, it is of academic interest only whether it was your timing or the race committee's timing that was actually wrong—the race committee is starting the race, and the flags count. So, make it a habit—even if you *know* your time is right and there are other boats ahead of you—to always look at the committee boat for the flag signals. If the recall flag is up and you have even the slightest suspicion that you might be early (ignoring your watch) go back and start over. You will lose only a few seconds, which is better than losing a race.

Under the current NAYRU rules, the start is normally taken at the mast, but provision is made that the race committee can change this if desired, and generally small boat races are started and finished at the bow. If the start (or finish) is taken any place except at the mast, it is supposed to be in the race instructions, but if you are sailing in a regatta away from home it is a good idea to make sure that the committee doesn't plan on taking the start at the bow, but forgot to mention it in the instructions. I have seen this happen—and a boat whose bow was over the line at the start was called back, although there was no mention in the instructions of the fact that the start would be taken at the bow. Under IYRU rules, if any part of the boat is over the line, it counts. For instance—under NAYRU rules a boat can reach down the line with its sheer over the line but the mast (or bow as the case may be) behind the line, and be all right—but not under IYRU rules.

Another good reason for reading the circular carefully when you are away from home is to be sure that you understand all the signals and can identify all the marks. Race committees at big regattas are very uncommunicative when they get on the water. When the signals for your race are hoisted, go over them with your crew to be sure that you have not made any mistake. Heading for the wrong mark or rounding it in the wrong direction can be very costly.

2. Starting to Windward

During the time between your arrival near the starting line and the actual start, make a careful check of the range through which the direction of the wind shifts, the frequency with which it shifts, and also determine whether most of the shifts are actual shifts or just apparent shifts due to increasing and decreasing wind velocity. Twenty minutes before the start, make up your mind on which main you will use if you have brought two. About 15 minutes before the start, check the tension on the foot of your main and on the halyards, heading the boat directly into the wind while you do this. Take one last look around to be sure that everything is buttoned on tightly and then get ready for the start. Raise your board and check the rudder for weeds if there are any around. You will by this time know the direction that you can sail on both tacks, and you should now reach down the starting line and get the compass bearing of the starting line unless other classes are using it—in that case, project out beyond one end or the other. During all of the time up to your final approach to the line, keep an eye on ɪne wind direction. Try a starboard tack close-hauled at least every two minutes and check your compass reading. A shift may make you revise your plans.

The installation of a compass should have been covered earlier under the subject of boat equipment, but there didn't seem to be a good place, and anyway many people think it is silly to put a compass on a small boat. It isn't—it's silly not to. Either a cheap airplane compass or an automobile compass is satisfactory. Neither will work at a very great angle of heel, but if you let the boat heel that much you aren't going any place anyway. The compass is very handy in trying to decide on which end of the line to start, but its greatest use will come up later. (There isn't as much skepticism on this subject as there once was.)

If the angle between the starboard tack close-hauled and the starting line is less than 45 degrees, the leeward end of the line will give a shorter course to the windward mark. If the line appears to be cockeyed, keep an eye on the committee boat—they can and sometimes do shift the line between the preparatory and warning guns, which may affect your starting plans. Also, in a high wind their anchor may drag which may result in a constantly shifting line.

In general, when the leeward end of the line gives a shorter course to the windward mark, it is best to plan to start on the leeward end of the line, *providing you have practiced starts and can time them accurately*. A late start on the leeward end of the line is apt to be extremely bad because you will either have to follow other boats for some distance or try to work through the fleet on a port tack which may be difficult. Incidentally, *never start on the leeward end of the line on a port tack* no matter how clear that end of the line seems to be, as a starboard tacker will always show up at the last minute and pick you off.

The only time that a port-tack start is safe is when it is impossible to cross the starting line on a starboard tack, and then be sure the race committee has not changed the line at the last minute (it ain't legal, but you are talking from the jail if they do and you get caught); keep your eyes open, and if you see trouble coming, avoid it before it arrives.

Sometimes special circumstances will exist which will make a start on the leeward end of the line inadvisable even if the course is shortest from this end and you have confidence in your ability to time your start accurately. In case it will be necessary to tack soon after starting to clear an obstruction such as a shore line or breakwater, or if it is a very short beat to the windward mark, it is probably better to start at the windward end of the line even though the course is longer from this end, as you will have less interference when it is necessary to tack. Also, sometimes the wind, tide, or water conditions are such that an immediate shift to port tack is desirable. You may anticipate a clockwise shift in the wind, such as frequently happens on Long Island Sound in the afternoon when the wind is a light easterly, or there may be a strong head tide and the port tack will take you close to shore where the tide is less or in a high wind you may want to go on a port tack to get close to a shore where the waves may not be so high. In these cases, the start should be made at the windward end of the line, even if the leeward end of the line gives a shorter distance.

The anti-barging rule has made the windward end of the line much more attractive for skippers accustomed to making well-timed, close-hauled starts, and it has also made this end of the line much less attractive for the boys who used to just hang around close to the line and then come in on a broad reach right with the gun. Barging itself is not illegal—if you can find a hole and sneak into it without interfering with anyone you are all right, but it's awfully risky business. The slightest interference with a close-hauled boat and you have no argument whatever—you are out. It is best not to try it. NAYRU and IYRU rules are together on this one now.

In a light wind, stay close to the line so that wind shifts or a drop in the wind will not leave you waiting a long way away from the line. Keep your boat moving, and keep your wind clear all of the time that you are maneuvering around before the start in a light wind. Do not sit around just bouncing up and down, as it takes even a small boat a long time to get moving at maximum speed in a light wind once it has stopped or slowed down. Keep your eye on the wind pennant to be sure that the wind has not shifted without your noticing it. In a light, shifty wind it is particularly dangerous to hang around the leeward end of the line—stay away unless you have decided to start there.

Remember that hitting the line at full speed with a clear wind slightly late or at a poor location on the line is much better than hitting the line early and having to luff to kill speed. The inevitable result of hitting the line early and luffing to kill speed is that later boats coming with full speed will carry on past you while you are trying to get started, and you will soon be blanketed. If there are lots of boats on a short line, it may pay to wait and get a fast start with your wind clear rather than to get bottled up with a mob of boats all blanketing each other. After all—it is where you are two minutes after the start that really counts.

In timing your start, cross the line in the reverse direction to which the start will be made, and read the time remaining when you are even with the point on the line where you will cross it on the actual start, not at the point at which you cross the line in the reverse direction (Figure 27). Divide the remaining time by two and add to this half of the estimated time to jibe or tack. This amount of time should be determined by practice starts before the race. On small boats the amount added will vary from about five seconds in light winds to two and one-half seconds with a wind of about eight to ten miles an hour to nothing with high winds. Adding nothing for tacking time in a high wind doesn't mean that the boat does not take some time to come about. It merely means that the boat goes faster on the beat for the line than it does on the reverse course, which is a very broad reach and the jib is generally not working very effectively, which cancels out part of all of the time taken to tack or jibe. The proper time to hit the line in the reverse direction

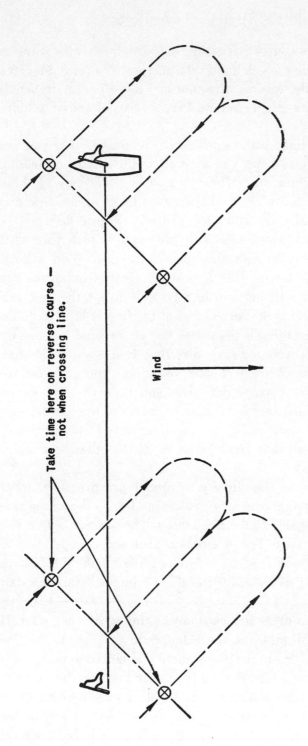

Take time here on reverse course — not when crossing line.

Wind

Fig. 27

When crossing the starting line (or an extension of it) in order to time your start, you generally do not cross at the same spot at which you will actually cross the line on the start. If you do cross it at a different point, sight directly across the boat and read your watch when you are even with the point on the line at which you will cross it later.

81

depends on the wind and the tactics that other boats are apparently going to use. In anything but a drifting match and in the absence of strong tides, the line should be crossed in the reverse direction at least 40 seconds before the start, but not more than a minute before. Larger boats of course require more time.

When approaching the line on the actual start, remember that you are crossing the line at an angle and that you must allow for that in estimating your position in relation to the line. There is a strong tendency to think you are closer than you actually are at the windward end of the line and farther away than you actually are at the leeward end (Figure 28).

If it looks like the race is going to be a drifting match, plan your start early because with no wind you can't make much progress. With a large number of boats and a long starting line, it is of the greatest importance to pick the end of the line that will put you in a position to get the first puff of breeze when it comes. Picking the correct end of the line is largely guess-work, but probably the safest thing is to assume that if the wind has merely died a bit, it will come back from the same direction. If it is absolutely flat, play for a pronounced shift. When you start your final approach for the line, be sure that you are on a course that gives you right of way—be on the starboard tack close hauled if it is possible to cross the line on the star-board tack. With no wind, your ability to maneuver out of another boat's way is severely curtailed, and it is much better to let the other boat worry about keeping out of the way.

You will probably have no opportunity to time a practice start under these conditions as there is too much chance of getting left on the wrong side of the line. Stay on the right side of the line close to the position where you have decided to make your start. Try to estimate your speed in relation to the starting mark, and don't wait too long before heading for the line. I have headed for the line from a distance of 50 feet three minutes before the start and still been late.

A strong tide will have a great influence on the timing of your start. If the tide is against you, it will take you much longer to get back to the line than it did to reach from the line to the place where you tacked to make your start. Also—the tide will have a big effect on the course that you can actually make good. With a strong head tide and light wind, it may be difficult or even impossible to clear a large committee boat on the leeward end of the line, especially if it is moored to a buoy and if you happen to be blanketed a little. If the committee boat is on the windward end of the line it will simplify the problems involved in getting across the line, but in either case,

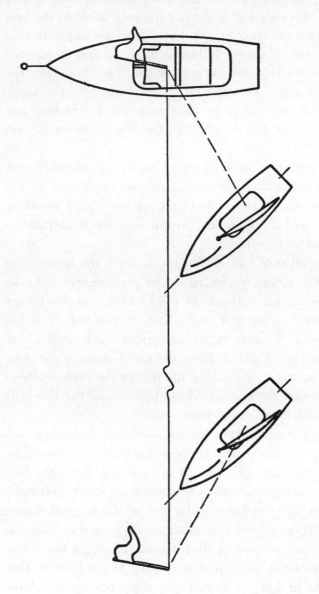

Fig. 28

Note that due to the relationship of the boat's course, the starting line, and the skipper's position, when starting at the leeward end of the line you will think you are later than you actually are, and at the windward end of the line you will think you are earlier (there is a strong tendency to just look across the boat at the flag instead of projecting the actual starting line from the flag).

with a light wind and a strong head tide, always hit the windward end of the line. Be late if necessary, but be right at the windward end. If your start happens to be timed perfectly you can just keep going or tack if you wish. If it doesn't turn out that way and you are following other boats, you can go onto a port tack and get clear at any time. Just the opposite rule applies with a light wind and a strong following tide. In this case, stay farther away from the line while maneuvering for the start, and take the leeward end unless the other end is far superior. If you must take the windward end, be sure you don't turn out to be barging at the last instant just because you did not allow enough for the effect of the tide (Figures 29 and 30).

Occasionally you will get starting lines going to windward when one end of the line is so much better than the other that you (and most of the others too) will have to start on the best end or take too much of a sacrifice. You know there will be an awful mob scene, so the problem is to make a start that is safe and as good as possible.

In the case where the windward end of the line is much the better, you want to cross the line as close to the windward end as possible, yet not take any chance of barging or being luffed above the mark. Also, you don't want to get caught much to leeward of the end of the line, as you will be hopelessly blanketed and you won't be able to go onto a port tack until about all the windward boats have passed you. If there are many boats in the race, you can't plan on timing your start by crossing the line in the reverse direction just before the start because the mob of boats approaching the line will look like the thundering herd in an old Western movie.

The thing to do is to get your bearing for the starboard tack, then sail the reverse course crossing the line right at the windward end sometime before the start when the congestion isn't too great. Sail back from the line for a minute or so until you can get a line on something by which you hope you can locate the same spot later—a house and a tree on shore, some stakes or buoys, or if you are starting a long way offshore, a guessed-at distance back of the line. Remember the amount of time it took you to get there and during the remaining maneuvering time, practice trying to get back to that spot. On the final run for the line, try to hit that spot just a few seconds later than you think you should, starboard tack, close-hauled, and going at top speed. This won't give you a perfect start, but if you are the third or fourth boat over and right at the windward end, you are doing all right. If there are any bargers, just keep going. If they don't know the rules yet, they might as well learn them then and there. (Figure 31)

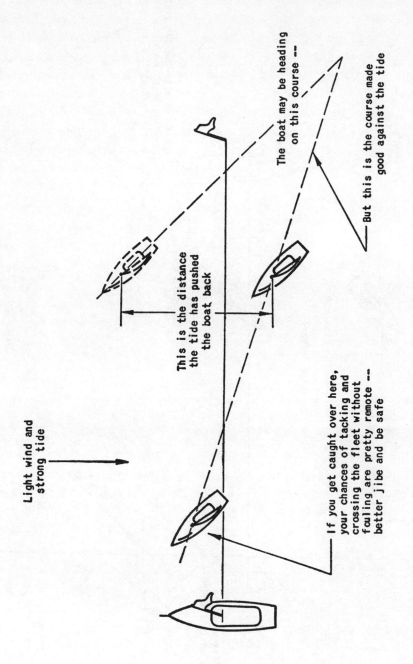

The boat may be heading
on this course —

But this is the course made
good against the tide

This is the distance
the tide has pushed
the boat back

Light wind and
strong tide

If you get caught over here,
your chances of tacking and
crossing the fleet without
fouling are pretty remote —
better jibe and be safe

Fig. 29

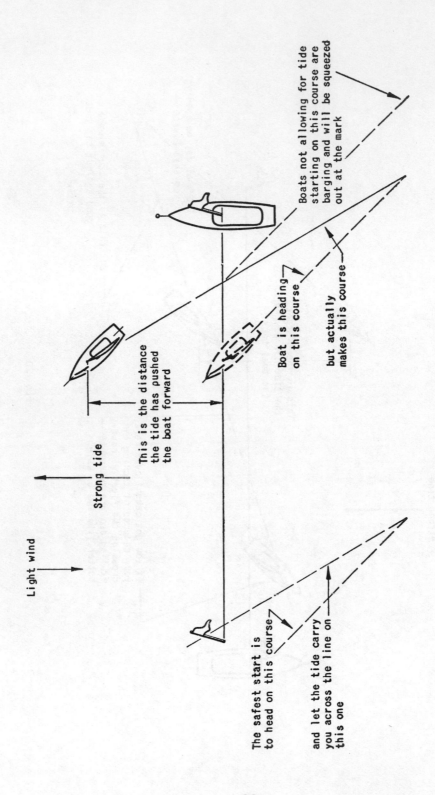

Boats not allowing for tide
starting on this course are
barging and will be squeezed
out at the mark

Boat is heading
on this course

but actually
makes this course

This is the distance
the tide has pushed
the boat forward

Strong tide

Light wind

The safest start is
to head on this course

and let the tide carry
you across the line on
this one

Fig. 30

86

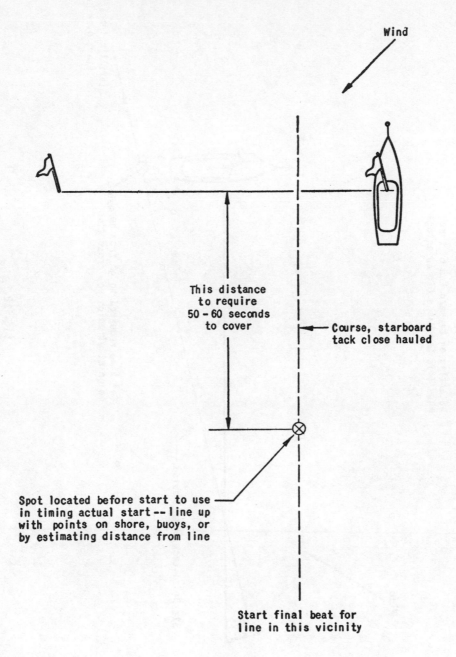

Wind

This distance
to require
50 - 60 seconds
to cover

Course, starboard
tack close hauled

Spot located before start to use
in timing actual start -- line up
with points on shore, buoys, or
by estimating distance from line

Start final beat for
line in this vicinity

Fig. 31

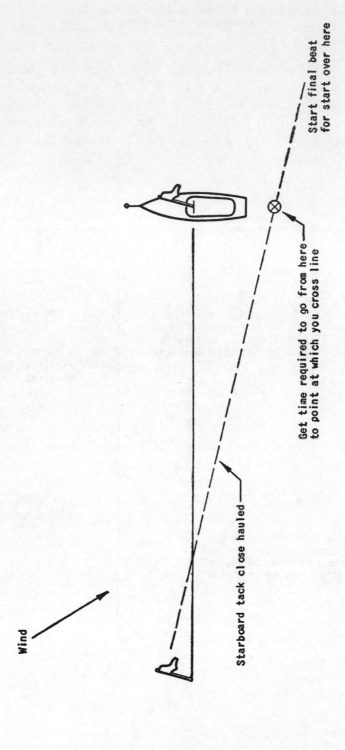

Starting on Leeward End of Line
When This End Has a Big Advantage

Wind

Starboard tack close hauled

Get time required to go from here
to point at which you cross line

Start final beat
for start over here

Fig. 32

88

The other case is where it is just barely possible to cross the line on a starboard tack. In this case, you will again not be able to time a start by sailing a reverse course just before the gun, because everyone will be in the same place at the same time. After getting your starboard tack course, take the time required to sail on a starboard tack, close-hauled from a point even with the windward end of the line to the place where you will cross the line near the leeward end and note how far you are behind the mark on the windward end of the line when sailing this course. Plan your start to arrive even with the windward end of the line, at the correct distance back of the windward end, between five and ten seconds later than you think you should in order to hit the leeward end exactly right. The reason for this five-to-ten-second margin is that a leeward boat might luff you a little and force you closer to the line than you would like to be. There will probably be some misguided souls who will be trying to hit this end of the line on a port tack. Yell as loudly as you can as it will only slow you down if you hit them. (Figure 32)

The advantages of these methods of starting when the lines are as illustrated are that you are assured of at least a fairly good start and freedom to tack soon after crossing the line, and also you tack or jibe to start your final beat to the line in an area that is not congested with boats; therefore there is less chance of fouling anyone when tacking or jibing, and less chance of being prevented by other boats from tacking or jibing when you wish to. These starts are of particular value when the wind is tricky and likely to shift at any time. They assure you of being relatively free to tack in case of a shift soon after the start. Also, poor starting lines such as we are discussing here usually happen as a result of tricky winds—it would be very seldom that a race committee would purposely lay out a line giving so much advantage to one end.

In making an on-the-wind start, it is *always* best to plan on hitting the line close-hauled. This is not only true on the windward end of the line, where the anti-barging rules will catch you if you aren't close-hauled, but also when hitting the middle of the line or the leeward end, as another boat which is to leeward of you may run you over the line ahead of time if you are trying to reach down the line.

There ought to be some rule against people getting to the line early and then sitting there with their sails flapping, not going anywhere, and making it difficult for later boats with a well-timed start—but there isn't. They don't gain anything by it as boats with way on will sail right past them, but you can't just run into them. They of course can't bear off on an overlapping boat, but the close-hauled, overtaking boat has no right-of-way just because he is close-hauled. His only right-of-way is by virtue of being the leeward boat—and in overtaking to leeward, he must allow the windward boat room and opportunity (time) to keep clear. And if the early boat is dead in the water, the overtaking boat can close in awfully fast and may find himself in trouble. If he is going too fast, his only out is to bear off to clear the dead ducks. Loud yelling is recommended, although probably no one will be listening. The IYRU rules differentiate between a leeward converging yacht which may luff gradually. Under NAYRU rules, the course doesn't enter into it and a leeward yacht must obey the overtaking rules.

3. Starts off the Wind

RACE COMMITTEES SHOULD BE LINED UP AND SHOT FOR STARTING A RACE OFF the wind, particularly if the start is running before the wind. Sometimes, however, it is either impossible or it is considered too much work to avoid a start off the wind, and a terrific mess is likely to follow.

Regardless of the distance between the ends of the starting line and the first mark, be very cautious in deciding on a start on the leeward end of the line when starting on a reach. A start on the leeward end is safe only if the wind is strong and steady and if your start is timed perfectly. Even if the wind is strong and steady and if it appears that the leeward end of the line will be relatively free from boats so that you can get an accurately timed start, it will still probably pay to start on the leeward end only if this end has a big advantage as far as distance is concerned or if this end will put you on the inside at the next mark and the next mark is fairly close.

If there aren't too many boats, the best start is to approach the windward end of the line close-hauled. In this way you have the right of way and have a great deal of freedom on the point at which you cross the starting line. If there is a large number of boats in the race, you may have difficulty defending your right-of-way and may get hit by a number of windward boats—all of whom you can disqualify if you can remember their numbers, and whom you can theoretically get to pay for the damage to your boat— but you can't do anything about the poor start you will end up with after being fouled.

In light airs it is almost never safe to make a start on the leeward end of the line when the starting course is a reach. No matter how well-timed your start is, you are almost sure to get bottled up. In light shifty winds when starting off the wind, it is frequently better to stay behind the line, keeping your boat moving fast and starting a little late near the center or the windward end, locating a clear spot and heading for it; it is much better to hit the line late and going fast than to hit it on time and be blanketed by other boats. If you do get bottled up on a start of this type, it is frequently better to cut behind a lot of boats and try to get upwind of them, rather than to stay in the middle of the mess even though you go a long way out of your way going behind boats to get upwind.

In starting a race where the first leg is directly before the wind, don't do the obvious thing and start directly before the wind. A broad reach is much faster than a run before the wind, and in addition, if you are reaching you will automatically be the leeward boat and have the right of way. The only time this is a poor idea is when there is a large number of boats starting and most of them haven't thought about starting on a reach. I tried it in Dallas one year with 36 boats in the race. It sounded like at least 18 of them hit me while I was trying to get unscrambled after a windward boat rammed me just ahead of the transom and headed me up into an involuntary luffing match with several other boats about two seconds before the gun went off. (Figure 33)

When the wind is light and fluky, a good downwind start is not particularly important as those behind generally blanket those ahead promptly after the start anyway. Unless you find a good clear place right at the start, you are just as well off to start a little late, with clear wind.

When the wind is steady, there is a good chance that practically everyone will arrive at the first mark at the same time after a downwind start. It is therefore a good idea to pick the end of the line that will put you on the inside at the mark, especially if the course is fairly short.

Downwind Starts

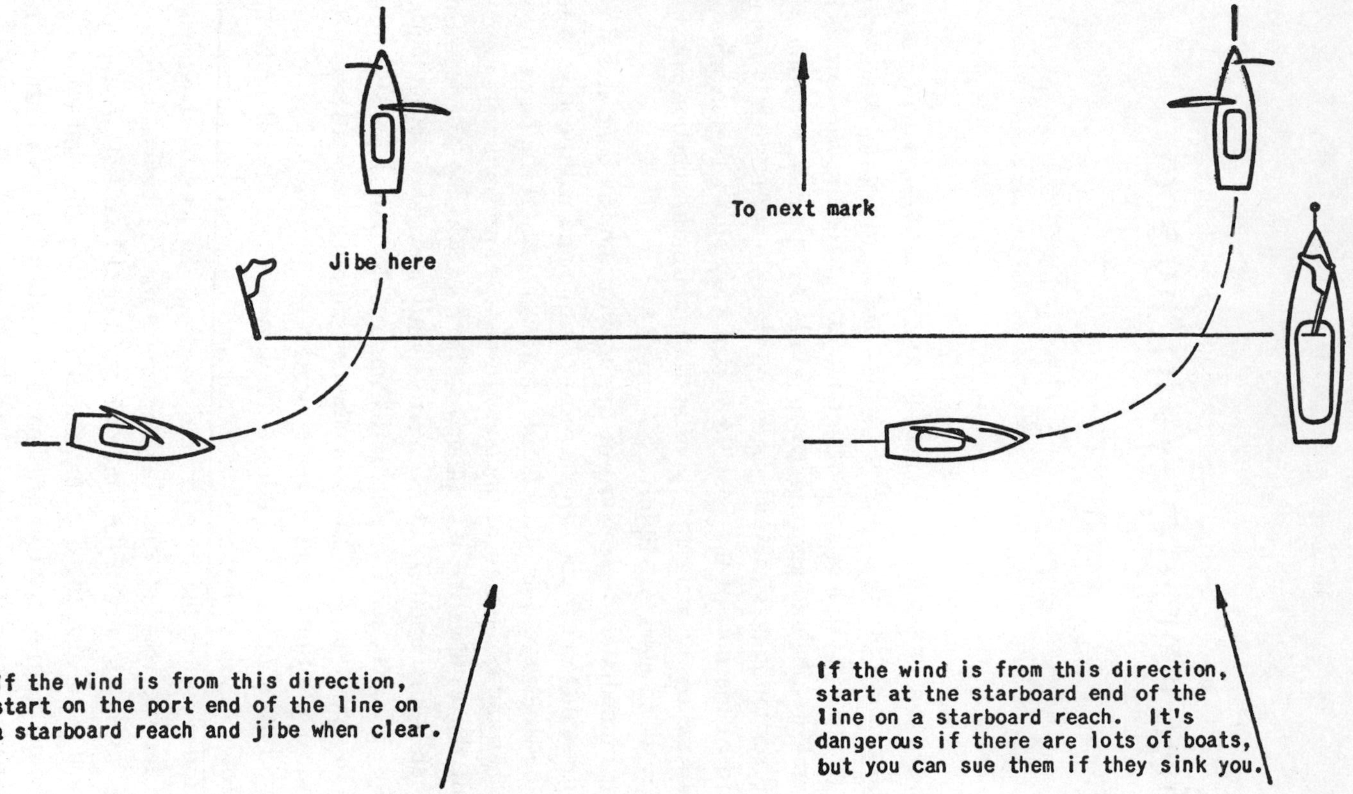

To next mark

Jibe here

If the wind is from this direction, start on the port end of the line on a starboard reach and jibe when clear.

If the wind is from this direction, start at the starboard end of the line on a starboard reach. It's dangerous if there are lots of boats, but you can sue them if they sink you.

Fig. 33

93

4. Beating to Windward

IMMEDIATELY TO LEEWARD OF ANY BOAT AND EXTENDING FOR A DISTANCE of about three mast lengths, there is a wind shadow where the wind velocity is greatly decreased. To leeward of the boat, except right at the bow, behind the boat, and even behind and slightly to windward, there is a region where the wind direction is noticeably changed and the velocity is slightly reduced. To leeward of the bow of the boat there is a very small region where the direction of the wind is deflected opposite to the normal deflection and where the velocity is accelerated slightly. (Figure 34)

A boat immediately to leeward of the bow of another boat and slightly ahead of it is said to be in the safe leeward position and will be able to forge ahead of the windward boat. This is true, however, only if the boats are very close together and if the mast of the leeward boat is approximately even with the bow of the windward boat; otherwise, a boat which is to leeward of another boat, behind another boat, or even slightly to windward and behind is in a hopeless position, and it is practically impossible to work past the leading boat from this position. Dr. Curry was the first author to call attention to the "safe leeward position," and it really works—but there are a lot of ifs, wheres, and buts about it. Theoretically the leeward yacht has the advantage when its bow is even with that of the windward one, but in practice that is cutting it too close. In the safe leeward position, the leeward boat has the advantage for two reasons—the slight acceleration and favorable deflection of the wind in the vicinity of the jib of the windward boat is favorable to the leeward boat, and also the deceleration and unfavorable deflection of the wind by the mainsail of the leeward boat is very bad for the windward boat.

The hopeless leeward position is hopeless because the wind velocity of the leeward or following boat is somewhat decreased, and also the deflection of the wind is such that the following or leeward boat cannot point as high. Except in the direct wind shadow the deflection of the wind is more important

The apparent wind is the resultant of the two vectors representing respectively the direction and velocity of the actual wind and the course and speed of the boat.

Boat-speed

Apparent wind

Actual wind

Wind Conditions Surrounding a Boat on a Beat to Windward

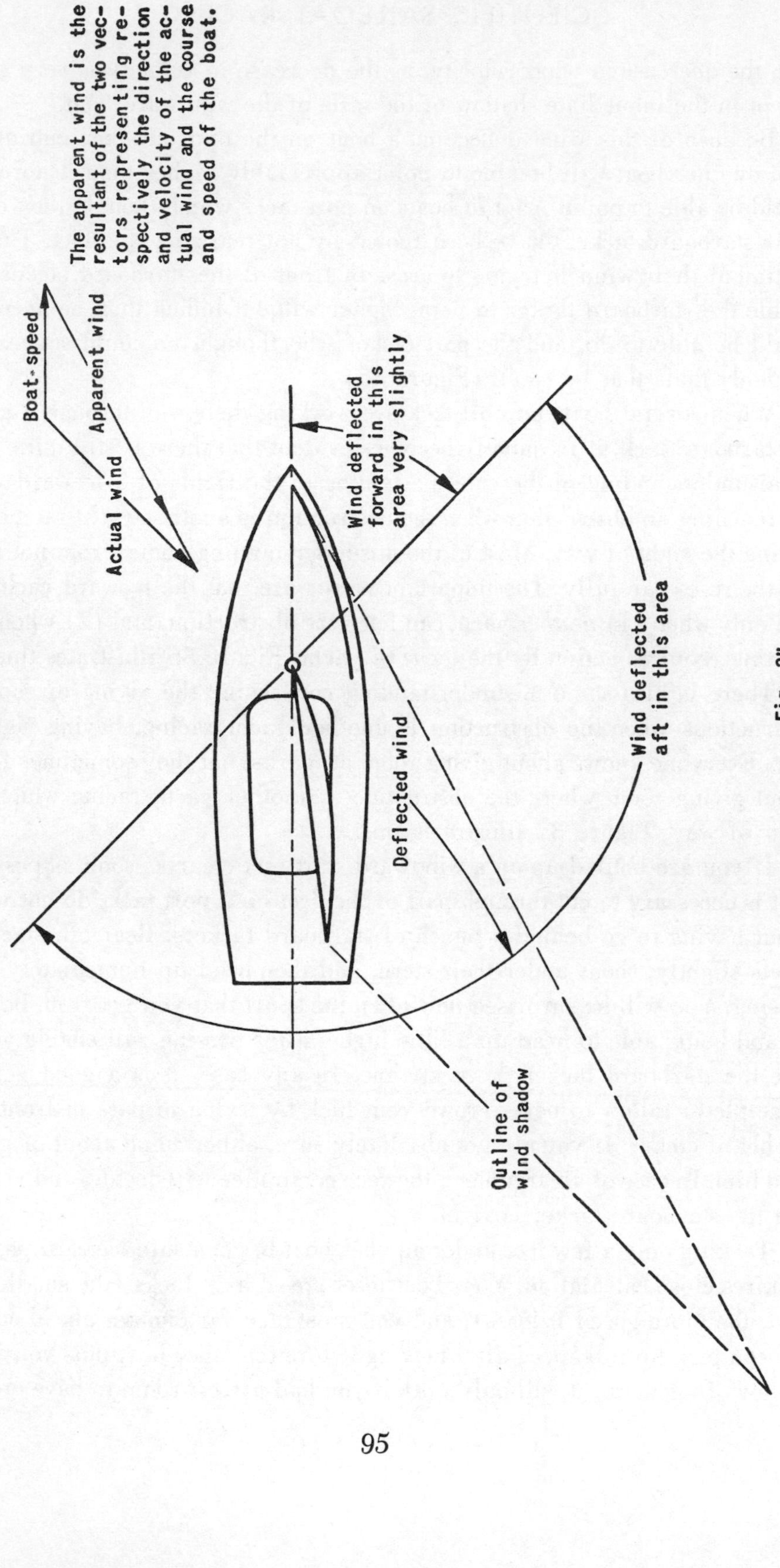

Wind deflected forward in this area very slightly

Deflected wind

Wind deflected aft in this area

Outline of wind shadow

Fig. 34

than the decrease in wind velocity, as the decrease in velocity is very slight except in the immediate shadow of the sails of the windward boat.

Because of this wind deflection, a boat on the opposite tack cutting behind another boat will be able to point appreciably higher than it normally would be able to point. A lot of boats on port tacks which thought they could clear starboard tackers have been fooled by not realizing this fact. The deflection of their wind in trying to cross in front of the starboard tacker will enable the starboard tacker to point higher without luffing than he normally would be able to do, and the port tacker who thought he could squeeze by suddenly finds that he can't. (Figure 35)

When several boats on port tack are working their way through a group on starboard tack, it frequently becomes evident that there is still quite a bit of misunderstanding of the rules pertaining to the rights of a leeward yacht approaching an obstruction when the obstruction is another yacht racing and having the right of way. Most of the misunderstanding comes from not reading the rules carefully. The important points are that the leeward yacht can hail only when (1) *neither* yacht can fetch the obstruction, and (2) when safe piloting requires action by the *leeward* yacht. Figure 36 illustrates this.

There is also some misunderstanding concerning the giving of room at obstructions when the obstruction is another yacht racing, having right of way. Everyone knows about giving room at marks, but they sometimes forget about giving room where the obstruction is another yacht racing which has right of way. Figure 37 illustrates this.

If you are bottled up on a windward start, get clear as soon as possible. If it is necessary to cut through part of the fleet on a port tack, do not worry about having to go behind a bunch of starboard tackers. Bear off, slack the sheets slightly, shoot under their stern, and then head up immediately after passing. You will be surprised how often the spurt that you get from bearing off and being able to head up a little higher after passing will enable you to take the starboard tacker the next time. In any case, it is a good general principle to follow to never crowd your luck by trying to pass in front of a starboard tacker. If you are not absolutely sure, either come about or go behind him. In case of an argument, the race committee will decide, and rightly, that the starboard tacker is right.

Tacking only a few feet under another boat to get a safe leeward position requires close calculation. Your boat loses speed as it tacks (the smaller the boat, the more speed it loses), and you must tack far enough ahead so that you can pick up full speed after tacking before the other boat puts you in his shadow. In general, it will only work if you had *almost* room to have crossed

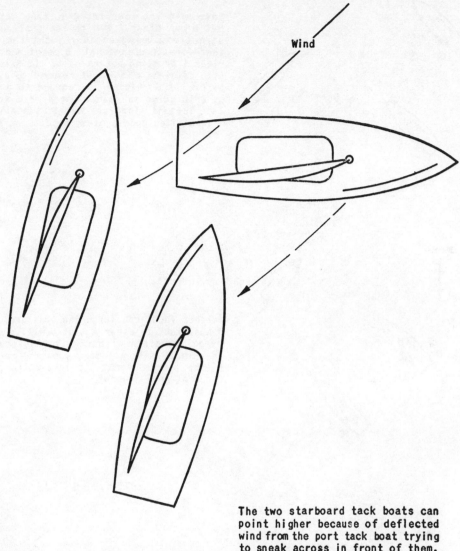

Wind

The two starboard tack boats can
point higher because of deflected
wind from the port tack boat trying
to sneak across in front of them.
This one didn't quite make it, although it probably looked as if he
could do it easily.

Fig. 35

97

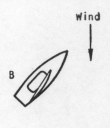

Wind

Safe piloting requires C to take action, but B can clear A (which ranks as an obstruction, being another yacht racing); therefore, C cannot hail B about and must clear A by going astern of A. If B is unable to clear A, she must respond to a hail by C. If B refuses to respond to a hail by C thinking she can clear A, and at the last instant finds she can't, she will be disqualified upon protest by C.

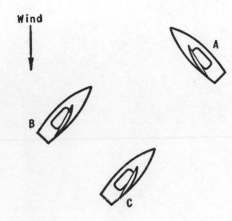

Wind

Neither yacht can fetch the obstruction A; B must tack to clear A, but C will clear A by going astern without altering course. Therefore, safe piloting does not require C (the leeward yacht) to take action, and C cannot hail B about.

Wind

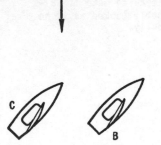

If Yacht C holds her course, she will clear A by going behind A. This probably would not be considered "fetching" the obstruction in the normal sense of the word and since safe piloting requires B to take action, C would have to come about upon a hail by B. If B should decide to go under the stern of A instead of tacking, C must be given room to clear also under Rule 3.

Fig. 36

98

Wind

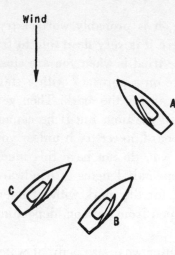

B can clear A by going astern, but must also allow C room to clear, as A is an obstruction, being another yacht racing, having right-of-way.

Wind

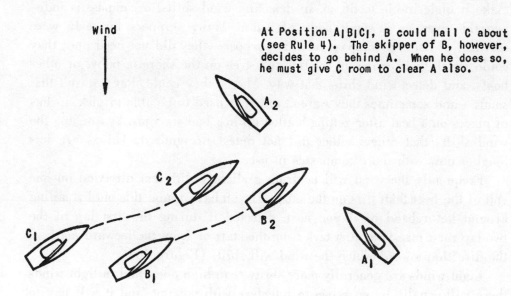

At Position A₁B₁C₁, B could hail C about (see Rule 4). The skipper of B, however, decides to go behind A. When he does so, he must give C room to clear A also.

Fig. 37

in front of the other boat. If you are this close, it is probably worth a try. There are, of course, special circumstances where it is very desirable to try it. The one situation in which it should *always* be tried is when you are close to a mark which is to be left to port and you are on a port tack with a starboard tacker approaching and you are sure he can lay the mark. Then you have nothing to lose by trying for a safe leeward position. But if he cannot lay the mark, or if the mark is to be left to starboard, *never* try it unless you have room to tack directly in front of him. If you do not have this much room, go behind him and tack about one and one-half lengths to windward of him. When you do this, he then cannot tack for the mark without interfering with you. Figure 38 shows what may happen from here on, depending on who thinks fastest.

All winds shift somewhat in direction no matter what size body of water you are on. They merely shift less often and through a smaller range on large bodies of water than they do on small ones, except in the case of very light winds and then no rules hold anywhere.

Figure 39 shows how only a very slight shift will alter the relative positions of two boats on opposite tacks. It is for this reason that it is necessary to detect wind shifts and tack with them unless some special circumstances make it undesirable to do so. In detecting wind shifts, a compass is indispensable even on a small body of water. Many skippers formerly were scornful of using a compass for this purpose—they did not need one; they could watch their course in relation to a tree on the shore, a buoy, or other boats, and detect wind shifts that way. Maybe they could, but I wasn't that smart—and sometimes they weren't either. I used to be able to pick up lots of places on a beat after getting bottled up in a bad start just by catching the wind shifts that others either did not detect or ignored. Things are lots tougher now with more compasses in use.

Frequently the wind will be from a slightly different direction on one end of the beat than it is on the other. If you have found this out by sailing around beforehand or if you have detected it during the first lap of the two-lap race, take your first tack from the start or from the leeward mark in the direction toward which the wind will shift. (Figure 40)

Light winds are generally more shifty than high ones, and in light winds there will usually be no waves to interfere with tacking, and it will pay to tack with every shift. Before tacking, however, be sure that the wind is actually shifting and that the shift is not just an apparent one from the wind velocity dropping momentarily. A compass is also helpful in finding out quickly whether the wind has gone around with you when you tacked, as it

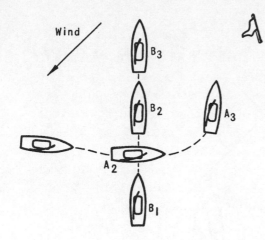

When B cannot lay the mark and A is not far enough ahead to try for a safe leeward position, A should go behind B and tack so as to be about one and one-half boat lengths to windward of B. B then cannot tack for the mark until A does.

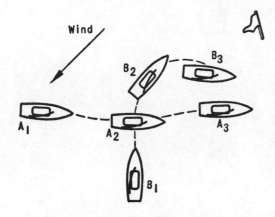

However, if the skipper of B is smart, as soon as A is under his stern, he will tack. He may fall behind A because A will be going faster, but if the mark is close, he can still probably prevent A from tacking until he tacks himself.

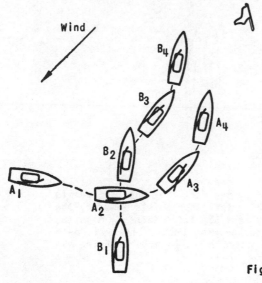

But if the skipper of A is still smarter, he will watch B and the instant that B starts to tack, he will tack (it's a good idea to hail too). Both yachts are tacking at the same time and B must clear A, B being on A's port side.

Fig. 38

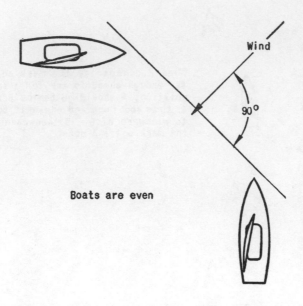

Boats are even

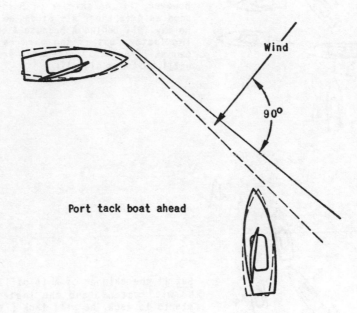

Port tack boat ahead

Fig. 39

The effect of the shift is compounded by the fact that one boat points higher by the amount of the shift, while the other points lower by the same amount. If we assume the wind shifts 5°, stays there 2½ minutes, and then shifts back, a boat which tacked with both shifts will gain 250 feet in 5 minutes on one which ignored them, both boats being assumed to be making 4 miles an hour.

102

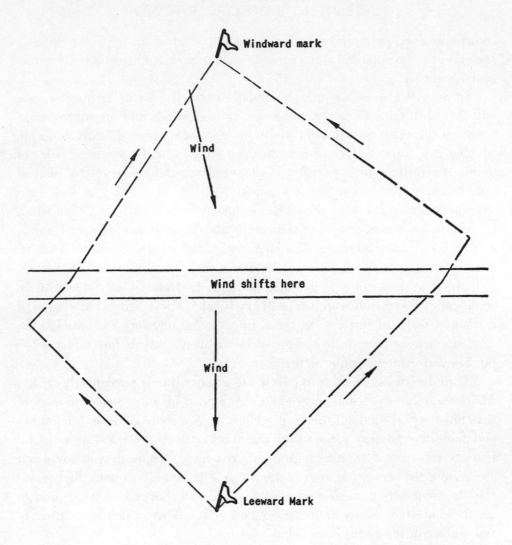

Windward mark

Wind

Wind shifts here

Wind

Leeward Mark

The condition shown above will frequently occur in the vicinity of a storm, on a lake near a point or a bend in the lake, or on a large body of water when the course is more or less at right angles to the shore. In the example shown, assuming the windward leg to be a mile long and the wind to shift as shown, the boat leaving the leeward mark on the starboard tack would beat the other one to the windward mark by 1000 feet!

Fig. 40

sometimes does, particularly when you have tacked on an apparent shift, as sometimes these apparent shifts precede an actual shift in the opposite direction. (Figure 41)

Shifts will also occur in high winds but usually not as frequently, nor will they shift through as great an angle. In high winds and big waves, more time is lost tacking than in light winds, and it is sometimes difficult to decide whether it will pay to tack or not when the wind shifts. Generally it will not unless the shift is quite definite. If the wind has definitely shifted against you, however, you had better tack quickly—the wind is likely to stay from the new direction for some time when it does definitely shift in a high wind.

If you know that you can't beat the boats ahead of you on speed alone, it may pay you to experiment in a long tack. If the wind shifts in your favor, you may pick up several places. If it doesn't shift, you haven't lost anything. If it shifts against you, you gambled and lost. Conversely, if you are fairly confident of doing well with just ordinary breaks, always go to the windward mark in a series of fairly short tacks. Come about on every shift, and if the wind doesn't shift for quite awhile, come about anyway before you get too far away from the middle of the fleet.

A windward leg which runs parallel to a shore line is particularly tricky. About the only way to find out whether it is a good idea to go close to a shore is to either try it yourself, or keep a close eye on someone else. Sometimes you don't dare go near a shore line, and at other times you don't dare not to. Usually you cannot point as high on approaching a shore as you could out away from the shore, but after tacking you will be able to point higher for a while. Generally the safest thing to do is to take short tacks not approaching the shore too closely until someone else does. Then watch him carefully and act according to the results he is getting.

If the wind happens to shift while you are close to shore so that you can sail a course straight to the mark parallel to the shore, don't be too jubilant, especially if the banks are high along the shore. This shift means that the wind is now crossing the shore line and anything may happen. Watch boats farther off shore carefully, and if they are moving faster, the quicker you swallow your pride and get away from the shore the better—even if you make what appears to be an unnecessary tack in order to get farther out, or bear off so that you will have to tack back later.

In tacking close to another boat don't assume that the present rules let you tack as you please. They don't, in spite of the fact that quite a few skippers apparently think so. Remember the other boat need not anticipate the necessity of clearing you. He can hold his course until you have com-

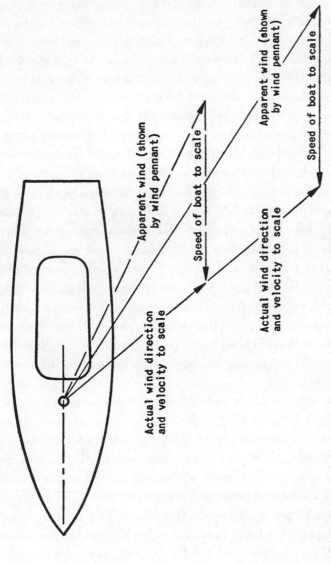

Apparent wind (shown
by wind pennant)

Speed of boat to scale

Apparent wind (shown
by wind pennant)

Speed of boat to scale

Actual wind direction
and velocity to scale

Actual wind direction
and velocity to scale

When the wind velocity drops momentarily, the speed of the boat remains constant because
of its momentum, and the apparent wind direction shifts, giving the same indication on
the wind pennant as an unfavorable wind shift. What makes these apparent shifts so
tricky is that they frequently precede an actual shift in the opposite direction.

Fig. 41

pleted your tack and your sails are filled on the new one. At that time, he must *start* to clear you, and you can't expect him to have a helicopter attachment to do it. The IYRU rules still have the "proper way" clause, which means allowing a bit more room than under NAYRU rules. And—don't forget—if you are the leeward of two port tack boats and are going over to starboard tack, yell loud enough for anyone within a hundred feet to hear you—*before* you tack. You aren't required to do this but it is a good idea anyway. Figure 42 illustrates the practical application of this rule.

Covering is done by staying on the same tack as another boat and either directly ahead or ahead and to windward. On a beat this is very effective, as it slows down the other boat and makes it fall off so that it cannot point as high. This effect only extends to about three mast lengths from the boat; however, if you are ahead, it always pays to cover your most dangerous competitor. Even if you are far enough ahead (four or five boat lengths) so that you are not interfering with his wind, it is still desirable to stay on the same tack so that he cannot get the benefit of a wind shift which you do not get.

However, do not waste time covering another boat which you know will beat you eventually. It is not only a poor way to win friends and influence people, but the inevitable tacking duel will cost you time which you cannot afford to lose as your own nearest competitor is probably merrily sailing along without any interference and will soon be hopelessly ahead of you. Of course if you are unfortunate enough to have won any kind of championship, you are fair game for everyone, and you can anticipate being covered by anyone within 150 feet.

When another boat tacks to cover you, the safest thing to do is to go over to the opposite tack while he is tacking, unless there are other boats around that you can't clear, or you are already fetching the mark and another tack would make you overstand it. If these circumstances exist, all you can do is make the best of a bad situation. If the other boat has crossed in front of you and tacked, slack your sheets and bear off a little and hope you get through his wind shadow before he picks up speed after tacking. Of course, if he is smart he will bear off too—it's legal now under NAYRU rules for a close-hauled boat to bear off on another close-hauled boat to leeward although of course the windward boat must not touch the leeward one—but the windward boat generally doesn't notice the leeward one bearing off, and sometimes you can break through (Figure 43). (The windward boat can't bear off under IYRU rules.)

If the covering boat tacks to leeward of you and far enough ahead to get a safe leeward position and you don't want to split tacks, there isn't anything

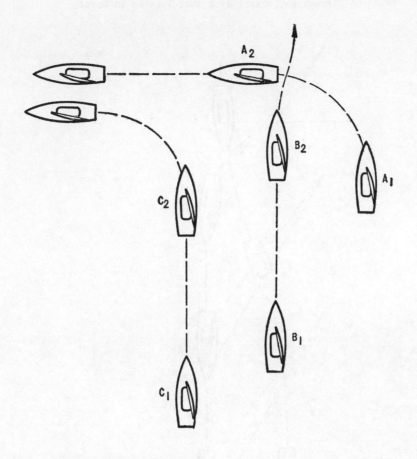

Fig. 42

A commences to tack at A₁ and while he is not required to hail, it is a good idea to do so anyway. A completes tack at A₂. At this time the other yachts must start to clear A. They do not need to anticipate the necessity of clearing A. B₁ and C₁ are the closest positions in which other yachts may be when A is at Position A₁ and still hold their courses to Positions B₂ and C₂ before starting to clear A. B bears off slightly and C tacks. Note that in the case of B, which is one boat length to windward of A, A must be clear ahead by one and one-quarter boat lengths when starting to tack. In the case of C, which is far enough to windward so that she will have to tack to clear A (two or more boat lengths to windward), A must be two boat lengths clear ahead. These distances are not necessarily exactly correct for any particular type of boat, but they illustrate the absolute minimum clearances that must be allowed. More is recommended to avoid being protested.

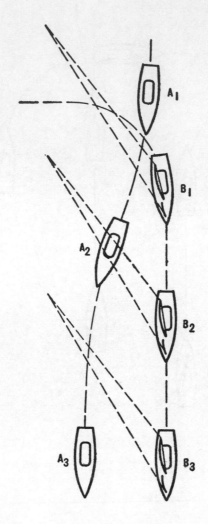

Fig. 43

B_1 has completed her tack just enough ahead of A_1 so A_1 can clear B_1. A starts to bear off as soon as it is obvious that B will tack in front of A and slightly to windward. The critical point is at Position A_2B_2 where A is directly in the wind shadow of B. If A can pick up enough speed by slacking sheets and bearing off while B is regaining speed lost in tacking to break through at Position A_2B_2, he will soon be clear as at A_3B_3. When this maneuver fails, it is generally because A was too far behind B at Position A_1B_1, or because A did not bear off far enough at Position A_2B_2. It is a difficult maneuver to perform successfully.

108

much you can do. If you aren't already laying the mark, you can try to split tacks when you are clear of other boats, but it probably won't do any good as the other boat will tack to cover you. If the two of you are well ahead, you can try to split tacks and if the other boat tacks to cover you, overstand the mark on purpose; then after tacking for the mark, bear off and try to go through to leeward. However, generally the best thing to do under these circumstances is just to relax and wait to get to the mark.

When trying to break through to windward of a boat which has tacked under you for a safe leeward position, remember that as soon as he has completed his tack, he has the right of way and you may have trouble keeping clear of him if his safe leeward position works. Don't wait too long to do something when you find that he has a safe leeward on you. If you tack soon enough, you may get clear. If you don't, you will have to luff in order to keep clear of him until you have dropped back astern of him. (Figure 44)

There is one place where pinching is good tactics. This is in case you are fairly well ahead of another boat, but to leeward. In this case you are not causing him much trouble, and you cannot tack without interfering with him. This is a good time to do a little judicious pinching—not too much—but enough to work up to where you are directly in front of him. He will, of course, be going faster than you for awhile, but as you get closer he will slow down and when you get directly ahead of him, he's through. (If he has his eyes open and recognizes what you are doing, he will start pinching, too—but usually he doesn't realize what is going on until it is too late.) (Figure 45)

If you are only a fairly short distance ahead of your most dangerous competitor, always stay on the same tack regardless of wind shifts. If it is toward the end of a regatta and he is the only one who can beat you, stay on the same tack with him and cover him no matter how crazy you think he is. If you are well ahead of him (over ten boat lengths), it is not necessary to stay on the same tack. Pick up your tacks according to the wind shifts, but always stay between him and the mark. Don't ever let him get off by himself where he might pick up a breeze that you do not get.

If you are covered by a boat which you know you can beat, do everything possible to get clear, but do not get excited and start overstanding marks or pinching the boat in the process. If the wind is shifty and you are covered by a skipper who is good at catching the wind shifts and it is early in the race, the best thing to do is to just resign yourself to being covered for the time being and wait to get clear later. If you are covered late in a race, occasionally a false tack—that is going halfway about and then coming back to the original tack—will work. If this doesn't work, try to maneuver your

Breaking Through to Windward of a Boat Tacking to Cover

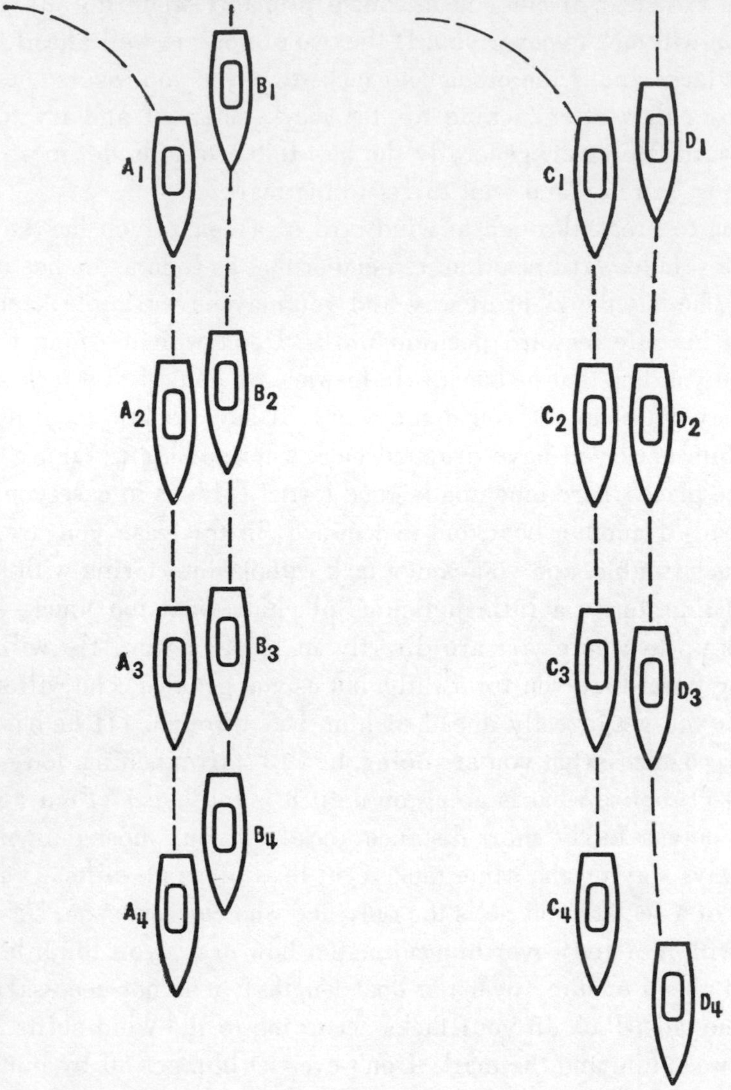

A₁ and C₁ have completed tacks under B₁ and D₁, hoping to get safe leeward positions. About all that B and D can do is to sail their boats as
fast as possible and be sure to keep clear of A and C which have right-
of-way, including luffing rights. At B₂, B should realize that he is
not going to make it. He will hold his own for a short while, then
start to fall back. Unless there are good reasons for not tacking, he
should do so. At D₂, D has gotten up to where his bow is even with that
of C. If D can gain a trifle more as at D₃, C is through.

Fig. 44

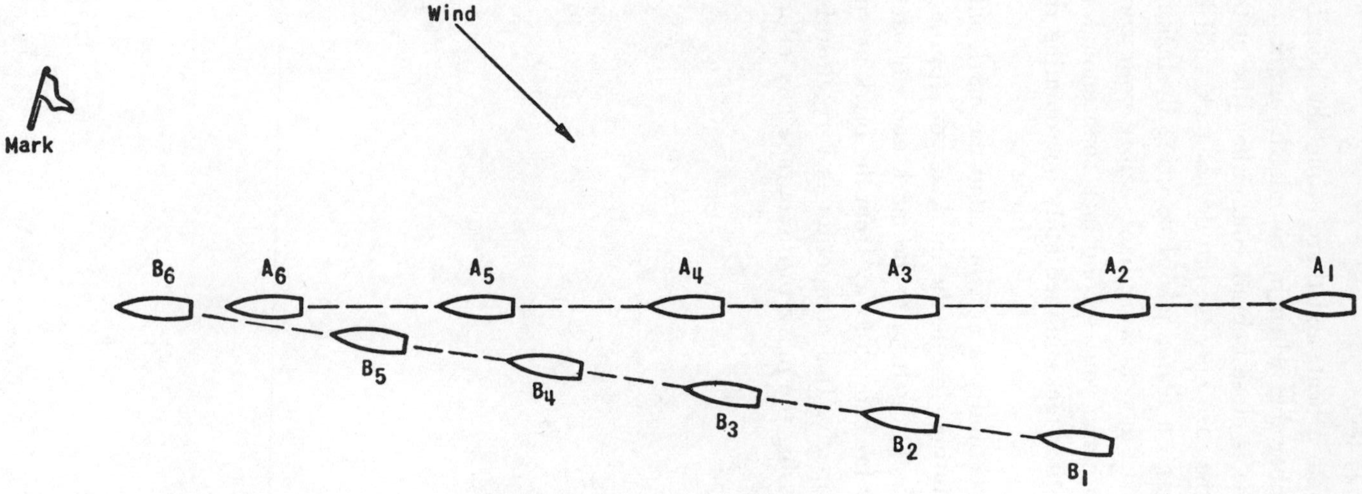

At Position A_1B_1, B is two boat lengths to leeward of A and three and one-half lengths ahead, but cannot safely tack for the mark as A is on a starboard tack and B would not be able to tack and cross in front of A. B, therefore, starts pinching a little (the amount shown in the illustration is exaggerated) sacrificing some of the lead over A in order to work to windward. If the skipper of A is smart, he will start pinching too, but he usually doesn't realize what is going on until about Position A_4B_4, by which time it is too late. Even if A then starts to pinch, all he can accomplish is hold about the same course as he has been sailing, as at A_5B_5 and A_6B_6, B is backwinding A badly.

Fig. 45

tacking so that you end up directly to leeward of the covering boat, then bear off a little and try to sail through his lee.

When rounding a mark going onto a beat, and there is another boat behind that you want to cover, remember that when he rounds the mark you must be on the same tack he is. If he is close behind you, either jibe at the mark or harden up on the wind as the case may be, but do not tack until he does. If far enough ahead, you can do a better job of covering by tacking once shortly after rounding the mark, then tacking back before your competitor rounds the mark. Be sure to make your second tack soon enough to be able to tack again if your competitor tacks immediately on rounding the mark. (Figure 46)

If your competitor is very close behind you as you round the mark onto a beat, don't let him suck you into cutting close to the mark as you approach it. If you do, he can bear off a bit before getting to the mark and cut back, ending up to windward of you. Stay far enough away from the mark as you approach it so you can round it properly. If a competitor is very close behind you, head up sharply after passing the mark to discourage any efforts to cut in to windward of you.

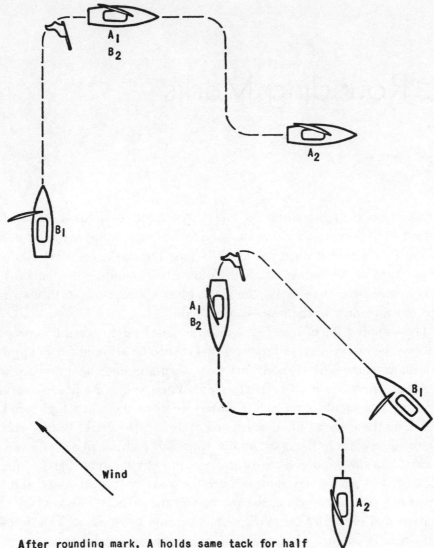

Wind

After rounding mark, A holds same tack for half
the distance between A_1 and B_1, then tacks. Just
before B reaches mark, A tacks again so that A is
at Position A_2 when B has rounded the mark to B_2.
If B tacks immediately after rounding mark, A
tacks at the same time to cover.

Fig. 46

5. Rounding Marks

MARKS SHOULD BE ROUNDED SO THAT THE SHORTEST TOTAL DISTANCE IS traveled in the process. This means staying far enough above the mark when approaching it so that when you actually pass the mark, you have made half of your turn to the course you will follow after rounding the mark. A customary error is in just clearing the mark when approaching it, then swinging wide away from it in the process of rounding it.

The sloppiest job of rounding a mark is usually done when it is necessary to jibe at the mark. A much larger radius should be allowed for in approaching a mark where a jibe is necessary than when approaching a mark at which any other operation is to be performed. When you must jibe a mark, the only time you should approach it closely is when there is a high wind and you are on the verge of jibing when you approach the mark. In this case it is wise to come close to the mark on the approach and not jibe until even with the mark, as the wind and the boat may take charge immediately after the jibe; and if you have stayed away from the mark on the approach and jibed as you are still approaching the mark, you may easily lose control of the situation and either hit the mark or not be able to round it. This is particularly true if you are planing as you approach the mark.

On a beat with high winds and big waves, do not try to cut too close to the marks. A wave may either throw you over onto the mark; or, if the mark is a light buoy or a rowboat, it may toss it over onto you. Also, a puff may heel you over so that your sail touches the top of the flagpole, even if your hull is clearing by a good margin. This same advice applies also with a very light shifty wind, as a sudden drop in the wind may make you drift onto the mark; and particularly if there are other boats around restricting your maneuvering, a sudden shift may put you onto the mark. In any case, always try to round the windward mark from a starboard tack. Even when you think you have a clear approach to a mark on a port tack, starboard tackers

114

seem to show up in droves out of nowhere to pick you off. Remember, the starboard tacker does not have to be close-hauled any more to have the right of way, which plugs up the port tacker's last legal loophole.

Usually even more fouls occur at marks than at the start. Everyone of course wants to get around the mark first, and things happen so fast that unless the skippers know the rules well enough to apply them without stopping to think, fouls are likely to result. The present rules are quite clear in most respects, but it takes a lot of studying to know in a split second just how they apply. If you aren't sure, stay out of the mess and look up the rule when you get home. The next time you will know it.

One of the few places where some argument may arise under the present rules is in connection with trying to force another boat to tack at a mark. The rules do not list a mark as an obstruction, therefore, a windward yacht cannot be hailed about just to permit a leeward boat to tack and clear the mark. However, *boats at anchor* and *structures* are defined as obstructions at which a leeward yacht can force a windward yacht to give room for the leeward yacht to tack and clear the obstruction, *if safe piloting requires the leeward yacht to take action and if the windward yacht cannot fetch the obstruction.*

The problem then is—when does a mark become an obstruction? It would seem that a large government channel marker would be an obstruction, but how about an eight-foot skiff with a flag on it? Or if not a skiff, how about a 20-foot run-about used as a mark? The best thing is to ask the race committee before the first race whether or not their marks are obstructions until the NAYRU has ruled on a protest. In most cases, if the leeward yacht must take action, the windward yacht can fetch the obstruction unless it is unusually large, so the leeward yacht couldn't hail the windward one about anyway—but some people use some awfully big things for marks. (Figure 47)

In Figure 48 I don't think there is any question but that the conglomeration of buoy, race committee launch, and unused stake boat would be considered an obstruction on the leeward end of the starting line. This race is being sailed under the International Yacht Racing Association rules, and the skipper of 7165 is in the process of getting himself disqualified because he can't fetch the buoy to which the race committee launch is moored, and has hailed 6877 and 5654 about. He should have foreseen this difficulty and jibed before it was too late.

If we assume that the start is being made under NAYRU rules, a number of interesting points come up. It appears that 5654 would have fetched the

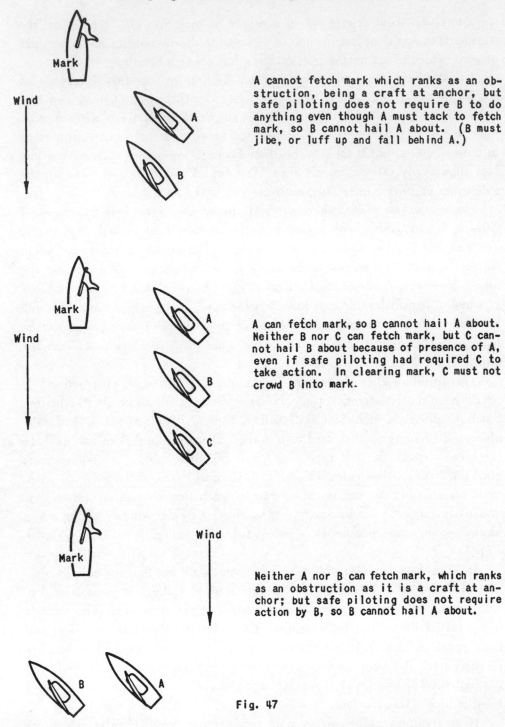

A cannot fetch mark which ranks as an obstruction, being a craft at anchor, but safe piloting does not require B to do anything even though A must tack to fetch mark, so B cannot hail A about. (B must jibe, or luff up and fall behind A.)

A can fetch mark, so B cannot hail A about. Neither B nor C can fetch mark, but C cannot hail B about because of presence of A, even if safe piloting had required C to take action. In clearing mark, C must not crowd B into mark.

Neither A nor B can fetch mark, which ranks as an obstruction as it is a craft at anchor; but safe piloting does not require action by B, so B cannot hail A about.

Fig. 47

116

mark, but that 6877 would not. Therefore, safe piloting would require 7165 and 6877 to take action. If 6877 could tack without interfering with 5654, 7165 could hail 6877 about; however, if 6877 could not tack without interfering with 5654, 6877 and 7165 would have to figure out some other way of getting out of the mess, as 5654 could fetch the obstruction and therefore 6877 could not hail 5654 about. The safest assumption to make if you get into a mess like this is that there will always be a boat to windward which can fetch the obstruction and that therefore you cannot force the boat to windward of you to tack.

Number 3291 is fetching the mark without difficulty, but it appears that 5212 might have a little trouble. Number 3291 would not have to tack if hailed by 5212, but if 5212 chose to luff around the obstruction, 3291 would have to respond to the luff and give 5212 room to clear the obstruction under Rule 3, even though the skipper of 3291 is well ahead of the mast of 5212 and 5212 therefore would not normally be allowed to luff 3291.

The unused stake boat tied alongside of the committee launch is about 12 feet long. Does this mean it will rank as an obstruction when used as a mark? I think it would—but I would ask the race committee before starting the race.

When the course is laid out so that marks are left to starboard, the starboard tack loses some of its advantages at the windward mark (Figure 49) if the port-tack skipper is smart enough. These situations will arise frequently on starboard courses, and are worth studying carefully.

It is never a good idea to try to lay the mark on a few long tacks, particularly if the wind is shifty. It is always better to save a short tack to use close to the mark. It is surprising how often you will find that you would have overstood the mark if you had not tacked earlier, saving another tack to use close to the mark. One exception to this advice occurs if you are being covered approaching a mark or if there are boats on the opposite tack coming up to the mark which will probably tack to cover you. In this case it is better to overstand the mark on purpose, as you may find yourself making a half dozen extra tacks as a result of falling below the mark from being covered. Or even worse, you will find it necessary to jibe in order to find a place in the parade. This can be very costly.

When you are approaching a mark on a reach or a run and there is another boat outside of you, be sure not to get clear ahead of the other boat at a point where he might be able to cut behind you and establish an overlap on the inside. Dragging your foot in the water was a very effective way of slowing down but it is now illegal. Also, be sure not to sail up close to the

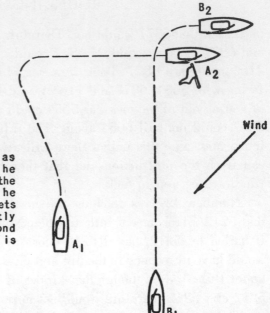

The skipper of A cannot tack when as close to B as in Position A₁B₁. If he keeps on, he will be carried beyond the mark until B tacks. A bears off so he can tack and hit mark just after B gets there. B does not dare tack directly in front of A so has to carry beyond mark before tacking (if B's skipper is smart, he will bear off with A).

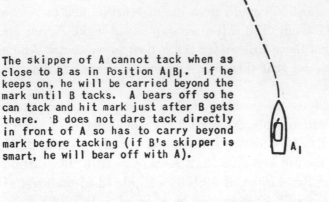

Wind

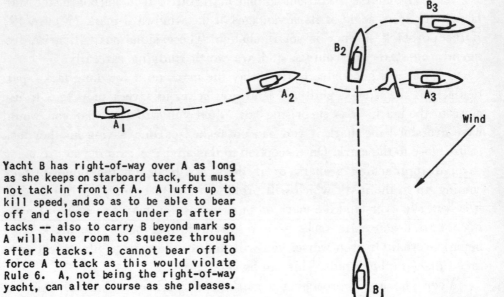

Yacht B has right-of-way over A as long as she keeps on starboard tack, but must not tack in front of A. A luffs up to kill speed, and so as to be able to bear off and close reach under B after B tacks -- also to carry B beyond mark so A will have room to squeeze through after B tacks. B cannot bear off to force A to tack as this would violate Rule 6. A, not being the right-of-way yacht, can alter course as she pleases.

Fig. 49

FIG. 43

Snipe 7165 is in the process of getting himself disqualified for forcing 5654 and 6877 to tack because he cannot fetch the buoy in front of the committee boat. This race is being run under the rules of the International Yacht Racing Union, but the photograph suggests some interesting possibilities for guessing what might have happened if it had been under NAYRU rules.

mark and then swing wide after rounding it, as the outside boat can then cut inside you. Insist on plenty of room to round the mark properly. When you are on the outside approaching a mark and fairly well back, swing out far enough so that if the other boat rounds the mark improperly you can cut inside of him. When doing this, however, you must be very careful as you are overtaking him to windward, and unless you head up just as fast as he does after rounding the mark you will be disqualified. Also, don't hit either the other boat or the mark as you have no right of way. You are taking a calculated risk and had better be sure you can make it before you go barging in.

Note that in tacking or jibing around a mark, luffing rights are determined by the relative positions of the two boats when the tack or jibe is completed. If the skipper of the windward boat is even with or ahead of the mast of the leeward boat, when the jibe or tack is completed, the leeward boat may not luff above its normal course. In this case, it is a good idea for the skipper of the windward boat to yell "mast abeam" to prevent any arguments.

However, luffing rights do not change merely because a mark has been rounded—that is luffing rights do not change between two boats rounding a mark off a reach or run when they stay overlapped on the same tack and merely head up on a beat. Several examples are given in Figures 50, 51, 52, and 53 of when luffing rights do and do not change at marks, and how they change when they do.

When rounding a mark off a reach or a run and going onto a beat to windward on the same tack, the sails must be trimmed and the boat headed on the correct course immediately. Any time lost sagging off below the correct course or even on the correct course with the sails flapping will almost certainly let a close competitor work upwind of you. It is best to have the crew pull in the jib and cleat it down for the beat just before rounding the mark, and then have him haul in on the main as you go around. After rounding the mark, head up closer into the wind than you think is necessary, even to the point of letting the jib luff for a moment. You should have a little extra speed left over from the reach which you can use to work to windward, and this will also discourage anyone who has tried to cut between you and the mark.

When you are on the outside approaching the mark and you are too far up on the other boat to make it practical to swing out and then try to cut inside, stay as close to the inside boat as you can safely until you have rounded the mark. If you see that you will be far enough up to get a safe leeward position, work up to windward all you can without sailing above

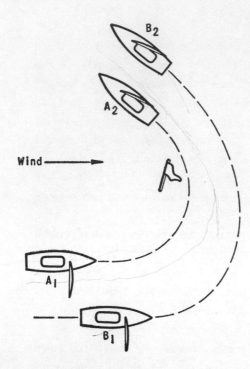

Wind ——→

When A and B round the mark without tacking and are overlapped all during the rounding of the mark, luffing rights do not change merely because the mark has been rounded. If B could luff A before rounding, she can still do so until the skipper of A is abeam of the mast of B. If B could not luff A before rounding the mark, she cannot do so after rounding as long as the same overlap exists.

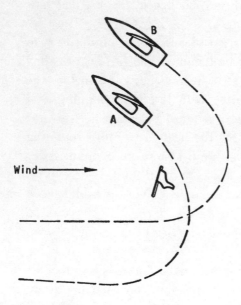

Wind ——→

In this case, both A and B have rounded a mark without tacking; however, A has been clear astern of B in the process of cutting inside of B and, therefore, a new overlap exists. B can now luff A until the skipper of A is abeam of the mast of B.

Fig. 50

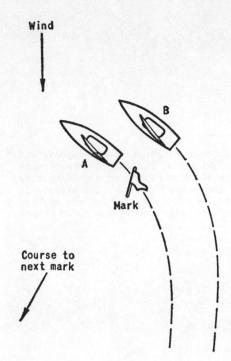

Wind

A

Mark

Course to
next mark

If A has luffing rights over B at the time
the mark is reached, A can carry B beyond
the mark if desired. However, if A does
not have luffing rights for any reason
(the skipper of B has at one time during
the existence of the overlap been abeam of
the mast of A or was ahead of the mast of
A when the overlap was established), A must
immediately upon rounding the mark head on
her normal course, which is for the next
mark.

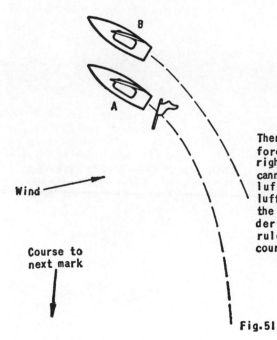

Wind

Course to
next mark

There is no circumstance under which B can
force A to tack here. If B has luffing
rights, she can luff A as she pleases, but
cannot force A to tack. If B does not have
luffing rights, she can still probably
luff A as her normal course is actually on
the opposite tack. A must not touch B under any circumstances, but there is no
rule requiring A to tack to her normal
course.

Fig. 51

121

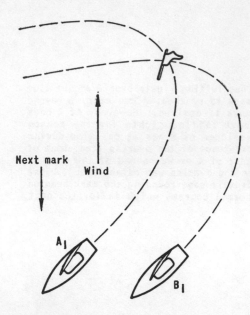

At I, B has rounded the mark sloppily and has tacked to port tack. A has rounded the mark close and has also tacked to port. When A completes her tack, the skipper of B is behind the mast of A, a new overlap has been established, and A has luffing rights.

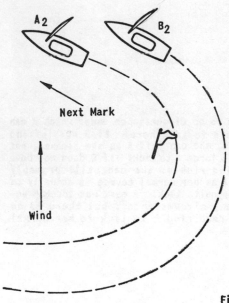

At 2, both yachts have jibed. When the jibe was completed, the skipper of A was ahead of the mast of B so B cannot luff.

Fig. 52

122

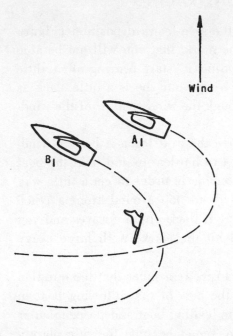

Wind

At 1, both yachts have jibed, with B cutting inside. In this case, A held too close to the mark before jibing, and at the completion of the jibe, the skipper of B was ahead of the mast of A, so A cannot luff B.

Next mark

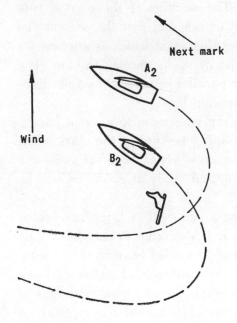

Wind

At 2, both yachts have jibed with A again holding too close to the mark before jibing. B swung too wide and cut inside of A, but the skipper of B is still behind the mast of A when the jibe is completed, so A can luff B.

Fig. 53

your normal course and do your best for the safe leeward position (Figure 54). However, if you see, as you round the mark, that you will not be able to get a safe leeward position after rounding it, start bearing off a little when you are half way around the mark. Keep your sheets a little slack as you continue to bear off and try to run through the wind shadow of the windward boat (Figure 55).

When rounding a mark off a reach when the next leg is a beat to windward on the opposite tack, it is a good idea to harden up and hold the boat close-hauled on the same tack for a few seconds in order to get a little way away from the mark. If an attempt is made to flop around from a reach onto a beat on the opposite tack, particularly if there are any waves and you have a light boat, it is likely to stop and hit the mark. With large heavy boats this will not be necessary.

When rounding a mark off a reach or a run, remember that the question of an overlap depends on the position of the bow of the following boat in relation to a line through the transom of the leading boat and perpendicular to the center line of the leading boat. Also, remember that the rule plainly states that in case of doubt as to whether or not the overlap was established in time, it will be assumed that the overlap was *not* established early enough. This rule was much abused in the past by yachts trying to establish an overlap and claim room at the last second. The working of the present rule indicates that the rules committee is tired of this and that the present one will give much greater protection to the leading yacht which is minding its own business and attempting to round the mark in normal fashion. The boats do not need to be on anywhere near parallel courses and do not have to be on the same tack at the end of a downwind leg.

Some skippers get confused by the rule giving room to a yacht having an overlap and try to extend that to permitting tacking at the mark when they please. The rules on tacking and jibing close aboard another yacht are entirely separate from the rule on sea room and apply at marks as well as anywhere else. See Figure 57.

When rounding a windward mark onto a run, with a large number of close-hauled boats approaching the mark, it is desirable to stay on a starboard tack for awhile until there are fewer close-hauled boats to tangle with. By staying on the starboard tack, only the starboard-tack, close-hauled boats will have right of way over you, which simplifies greatly your problems in getting back through the fleet. Also, give the close-hauled boats plenty of room. If the close-hauled boat just thinks he had to bear off, you may have trouble proving that he didn't if you cut it close. Theoretically, the boat

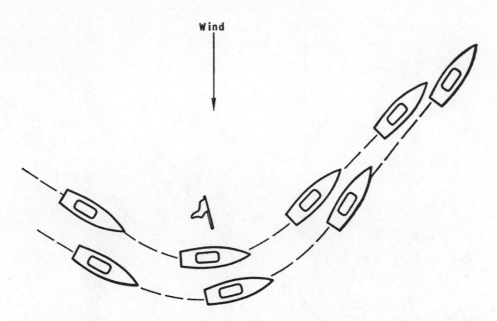

Getting a safe leeward position on a beat after rounding a mark from a reach.
Leeward boat must not head above normal course unless it had luffing rights
before rounding mark. The bow of the leeward boat must stay ahead of the bow
of the windward boat all the time during the rounding of the mark for this
maneuver to be successful, and the leeward one must stay as close as possible
to the windward one.

Fig. 54

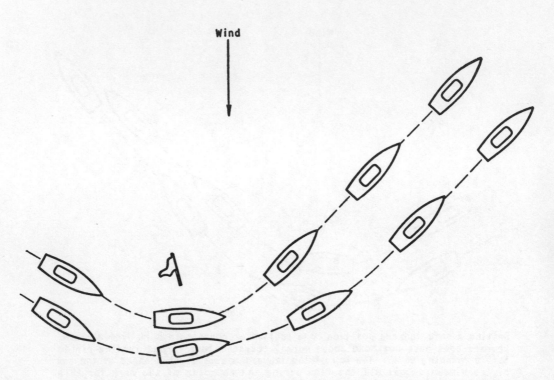

Wind

When it is apparent that a safe leeward position will be impossible, the leeward boat
bears off just enough to keep its wind clear. If it is faster than the windward boat, it
will gradually draw ahead and then, by pinching a trifle, can backwind the windward boat.
The pinching must not be started until the leeward boat is clear ahead of the windward
one or it will not be successful.

Fig. 55

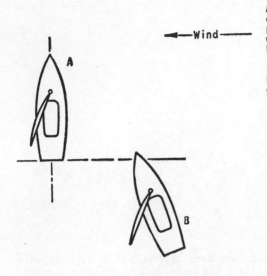

← Wind →

A must give B room at the mark if the overlap was established in time. The position shown is probably the latest that would be considered reasonable. If A had been farther to windward and the overlap had been established at the position shown, A would probably be considered as being too close to the mark to be able to give room.

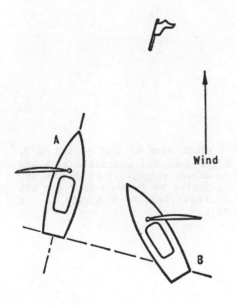

Wind ↑

B in this case can claim room even though A is on starboard tack. The starboard tack loses its right-of-way in the case of an overlap at the mark terminating in the downwind leg.

Fig. 56

127

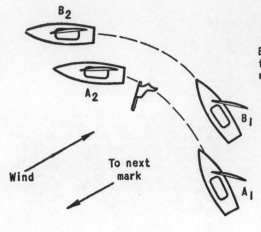

B must give A room at the mark, and cannot tack after rounding the mark until A has rounded and has tacked.

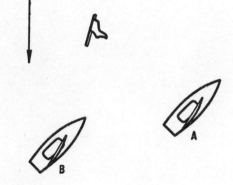

A cannot tack in front of B. A must wait until B has tacked before doing so herself.

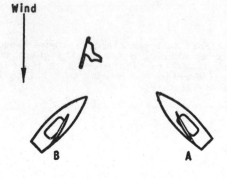

B cannot claim room to tack at the mark, Yacht A being on the starboard tack has the right-of-way regardless of whether she is close-hauled or running free for the mark and regardless of who gets to the mark first.

Fig. 57

128

running free might be considered the leeward boat if the close-hauled boat would just barely touch the transom of the boat running free. I don't believe this would be upheld on a protest, however.

When rounding a mark onto a run and the jib after rounding the mark onto the run will be on the same side as it is before rounding, some time can be saved by clipping the pole onto the jib sheet before rounding the mark and putting the pole out just as the mark is rounded. Don't try this in a high wind or if there is any doubt about whether the next leg is a close or broad reach.

6. Sailing on the Free Legs of the Course

WHEN REACHING AND PRESSED BY OTHER BOATS CLOSE BEHIND, IT IS DIFFI-cult to choose the best tactics. In general, it is best to stay directly ahead of the boat immediately behind you, particularly if he is your most dangerous competitor. However, if there is still another boat close behind and he is smart, he will bear off to get clear wind and is very likely to get to the next mark first or at least on the inside with an overlap if you head very far upwind. If you bear off and try to stay in front of him, the boat immediately behind you is likely to handen up on the wind and be able to shoot up just enough to blanket you. If it is a fairly close reach and the wind may shift against you, it is best to stay pretty well to windward. Falling below the mark and having to tack for it will be fatal.

When covering on a reach or a run, remember that the region in which you are taking another boat's wind extends about three mast lengths to leeward in the direction of the *apparent* wind. This looks complicated on paper, but on the water it is simple—your wind pennant is pointing in the direction of your wind shadow (Figure 58).

The best thing to do is to decide who is the most dangerous competitor in the end and try to stay ahead of him. In any case, do not get enticed into a luffing match. The only person who wins in a luffing match is the third man back who did not get into the match, except in very rare circumstances. The present rules make the boat overtaking another boat rapidly, such as if you should start planing a little before he does, or if you should get a puff in light air before he does, you can probably get up to where you are abeam of his mast before he can run you far off course. If you are overtaking slowly and he luffs gradually, you had better try the other side unless you

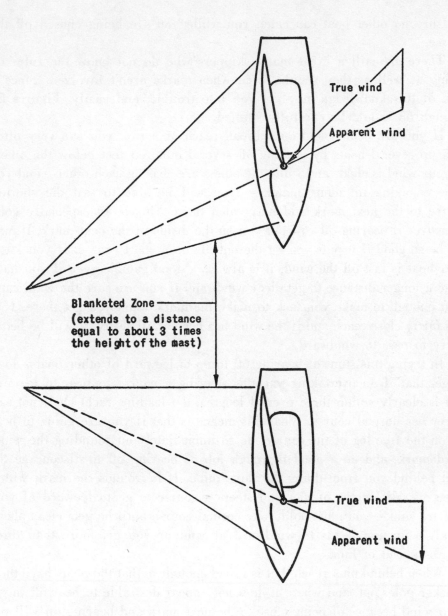

True wind

Apparent wind

Blanketed Zone
(extends to a distance
equal to about 3 times
the height of the mast)

True wind

Apparent wind

Fig. 58

are sure no other boat can catch you while you are being chased off the course.

There are still a great many skippers who do not know the rules on luffing as well as they should, even when marks aren't involved. Since a lack of this knowledge may get you into trouble, and easily, Figures 59 through 63 should be carefully studied.

If you are behind and on a broad reach or a run, you can very often pick up several boats by bearing off several hundred feet below the others so your wind is clear, and while the others are chasing each other—and you hope engaging in luffing matches—you will be able to sail the shortest course to the next mark and may catch them. This is an especially good maneuver if bearing off will put you on the inside of the next mark. It may not be so good if it puts you on the outside on a short course. If you know your boat is fast off the wind, it is always a good gamble even if you have to go a longer distance to get clear wind, and if you are sure the wind can't shift enough to make you tack to make the mark when you get there. If it is a fairly close reach and if the wind has been at all shifty, it will be better to try to pass to windward.

In trying this stunt of bearing off to go to leeward of other boats, don't forget that if an overtaking yacht is steering a course to pass to leeward and is clearly within three overall lengths, the leading yacht shall not sail below her normal course. What this means is that if you are going to bear off on the free leg of the course, do so immediately on rounding the windward mark, and do a good thorough job of bearing off to discourage the boat behind you from doing the same thing. If he rounds the mark within three overall lengths of you and steers a course to go to leeward of you, you are sunk—you must hold your normal course until he gets clear ahead or gives up and heads to windward of you, or you get more than three lengths ahead of him.

When behind on a reach that is broad enough so that the boats have their whisker poles out, and where it does not appear desirable to bear off to get clear wind because of being close to the next mark and bearing off will put you on the outside at the mark, you can frequently catch the boat ahead of you by gradually working upwind until only a few degrees from the point where the jib will not draw well. Inform your crew that as soon as he sees the tiller move he is to get the pole in and trim the sheets on the opposite side without your saying anything. Then when you are quite close to the boat ahead, and at a moment when he is not watching you, head up sharply. The chances are that he will try to luff you and in the process his jib will

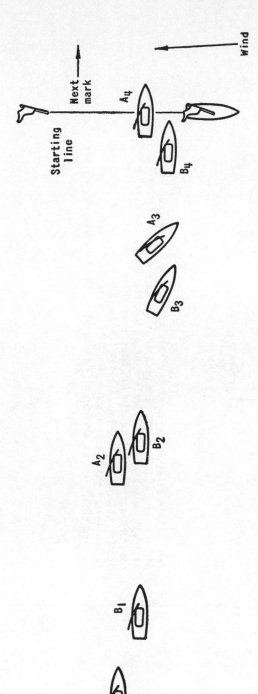

This example commences before the starting gun. At Position I, A is clear astern of B, overtaking B. At Position 2, A has overtaken B to leeward but may not luff B until the mast of A is ahead of the skipper of B, at which time A can luff gradually. At Position 3, the gun goes off. A must immediately head for the next mark as she cannot head above the course to the next mark until after the starting line is crossed. In Position 4, A having crossed the starting line with the skipper of B behind the mast of A, may again luff B.

Fig. 59

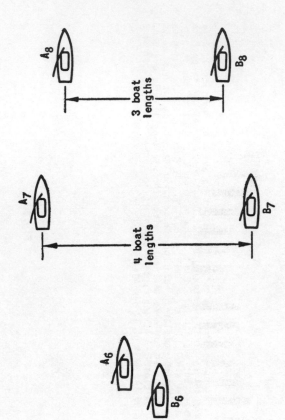

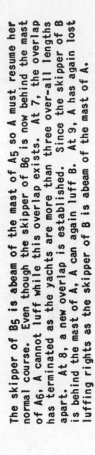

The skipper of B5 is abeam of the mast of A5 so A must resume her normal course. Even though the skipper of B6 is now behind the mast of A6, A cannot luff while this overlap exists. At 7, the overlap has terminated as the yachts are more than three over-all lengths apart. At 8, a new overlap is established. Since the skipper of B is behind the mast of A, A can again luff B. At 9, A has again lost luffing rights as the skipper of B is abeam of the mast of A.

Fig. 60

134

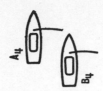

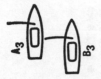

Wind

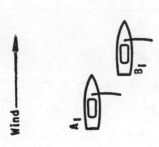

At Position A_2B_2, the skipper of A is ahead of the mast of B and B must therefore resume her normal course. At Position A_3B_3, both boats jibe. B is now the windward boat and as the skipper of B is behind the mast of A, A can luff B. At A_4B_4, both yachts have jibed again. This time the skipper of A is ahead of the mast of B at the time the jibe is completed, and therefore, B cannot luff A.

Fig. 61

135

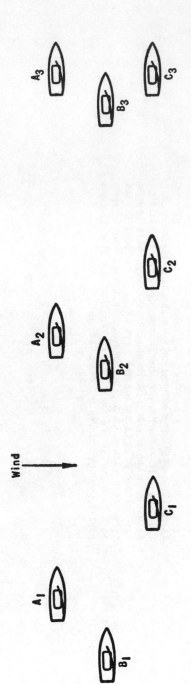

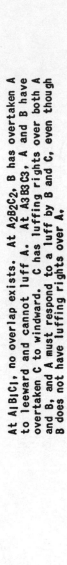

At $A_1B_1C_1$, no overlap exists. At $A_2B_2C_2$, B has overtaken A to leeward and cannot luff A. At $A_3B_3C_3$, A and B have overtaken C to windward. C has luffing rights over both A and B, and A must respond to a luff by B and C, even though B does not have luffing rights over A.

Fig. 62

136

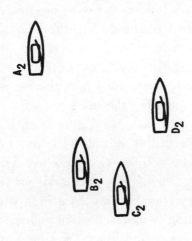

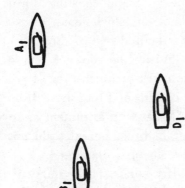

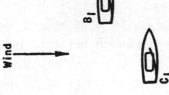

Wind →

At A₁B₁C₁D₁, no overlap exists. At A₂B₂C₂D₂, C has overtaken B and both are about to overtake D. At A₃B₃C₃D₃,
B and C have overtaken D to windward which would give D
luffing rights over both B and C. However, all three yachts
have overtaken A to leeward and none of them have luffing
rights on A. D may luff B and C only until they would interfere with A.

Fig. 63

137

collapse and the crew not being warned will bungle the job of getting the pole in. Then you have him.

If there is a mob of boats closely bunched approaching a mark on a broad reach or a run, it is better to be inside and behind than well up front and outside. This is particularly important as the inside position is the windward position after rounding the mark and boats which were well behind you but inside may end up ahead of you after rounding the mark. If you see that this is likely to happen, the best thing to do is to drop back and cut through the mob of boats going behind as many as necessary, but in any case get on the inside before you reach the mark. The three photographs, Figures 64, 65, and 66, are telephoto shots taken one after the other at a leeward mark and afford an interesting study on who got around the leeward mark first and why. Note that the outside boats must be quite far ahead of the inside ones to end up ahead after rounding the mark.

When trying to catch another boat on a run, blanketing is effective only when you are fairly close, and the wake of the boat ahead is quite effective in slowing down the following boat. In a light wind you can frequently catch a leading boat better by staying out of his wake and not trying to blanket him, at least until you are very close to him. In a high wind, particularly if planing is possible, blanketing is more effective and the wake is less effective. Once in awhile, in a good strong breeze, a slower boat can get a free ride behind a faster one which has just passed the slow one by getting on the stern wave of the leading boat and coasting down it. This works particularly well if a larger but not too much faster class is racing at the same time and you can hook a ride behind one of them.

When approaching a mark or the finish line, do not try to blanket another boat when too far away from the mark or finish line. If you blanket him too early, you may get clear ahead of him and then he will go to work on you. Do not wait so long that you will have an argument as to whether your overlap at a mark was established in time, but also do not start so early that you draw clear ahead and are in turn blanketed.

When running before the wind in shifty winds, particularly if they are light, jibe as often as necessary, as a good jibe can be done without losing any speed. A clip on the end of the whisker pole which holds the pole to the jib sheet is essential to efficient jibing. The crew should pull the pole back and put it out on the other side while the skipper handles the jib sheets. In a light wind the crew can do this with one hand and throw the boom over with the other hand. Jibing with a spinnaker can be done just about as fast, if you have proper equipment. Release the forward guy after the sheet has been slacked, if necessary, so that the end of the pole can be reached. In the meantime the skipper heads the boat slowly out of the wind. The pole is then removed from the fitting on the mast, the forward guy is attached to it (if you have provision to do this), and the pole is then attached to the former clew of the spinnaker which now becomes the tack. The opposite end of the pole is released from the former tack of the spinnaker, and as the boom swings over, the pole is attached to the mast, the sheets are trimmed, and practically no speed has been lost.

Some authorities recommend tacking when going downwind, so that the boat is never running directly before the wind. Admittedly, the position directly before the wind is the slowest point of sailing—but a straight line is still the shortest distance between two points. It is my opinion that ordinarily nothing is gained by tacking downwind, but also that within limits nothing will be lost either. If the wind velocity is marginal for planing and you can get the boat to plane by heading up a little from the course dead before the wind, it will really pay to go fairly far off course. If you can plane just as well directly before the wind, it won't pay. Tacking downwind and with an appreciable tide is another story, which will be covered later.

On a reach there are two times when following the shortest distance won't make the shortest time. These are when the wind is very puffy and either quite light or quite heavy. Under these conditions, it pays to head fairly far upwind during the lulls and bear off on the puffs. In a light puffy wind, this enables you to get the puffs sooner and ride them longer. In a wind that is just high enough for planing, you can plane with less wind while heading up, and then when the puff comes along, you can continue planing while bearing off and getting back to your normal course.

When running before the wind, remember that the starboard tack always has right of way. If you are on a port tack and are being overtaken by a boat on starboard tack, even though he is on your windward side, he has the right of way. You must either jibe over to a starboard tack yourself, or else figure out how to keep clear of him by some other means (unless you are about to round the leeward mark, in which case the starboard-tack boat loses its right of way).

7. Drifting Matches

A RACE WHEN THE WIND VARIES FROM NOTHING AT ALL TO VERY LITTLE more and shifts all over the compass is very appropriately known as a drifting match. About the only good advice I can give to one facing a drifting match is to give up sailing and take up outboard motor racing. The only thing you can be sure of is that 90 percent of what you do will seem to be wrong, unless you are in the lead. Then it will be 100 percent. Sometimes local knowledge helps, but even that backfires about as often as it works.

If you are on a beat, tack with every shift so as to always be on the tack heading closest to the mark, but if you see a better-than-average puff get into it as soon as possible even if you will not be on the tack heading closest to the mark. Sometimes the puffs travel along the water, and if you see ripples on the water in the direction from which the wind is coming, you can count on it getting to you. Other times, however, the wind seems to go straight up in the air after reaching a certain line and never moves across the water. If the puff is the type that moves and you are on a beat, you will get it about as soon on one tack as on the other. However, if the puff seems to be the stationary variety and it isn't too far away it will pay you to tack and go for it—or to bear off and reach for it if it looks like a good one, but doesn't seem to be moving.

Shore lines are particularly tricky during drifting matches. Generally they are dangerous, but you still have to watch them carefully as once in a great while a breeze will come along close to a shore and never get far away from the shore. When sailing against a strong tide in a drifting match, the decision on how close to go to a shore becomes especially important. If the ripples on the water indicate that the breeze is about as good close to shore, it will pay to get there as fast as possible, tacking away from the mark or bearing off from a beat to a reach as the case may be in order to get into the slower tide as quickly as possible. If this condition exists before the start of

140

the race, it should be the deciding factor in deciding on how to make your start. If your speed through the water is practically nothing, it will pay to completely ignore your normal course for a long enough time to get over to where the tide is less if you can then go in the general direction of the mark.

On a reach in a drifting match, it is a good idea to stay well upwind. Bearing off to try to pass a bunch of boats is quite hazardous, as the boats to windward get the puffs first and can ride them longer and the puffs frequently seem to fizzle out before they get very far down to leeward. Reaching along a shore line with an off-shore breeze presents a nice problem in trying to decide how far upwind and therefore how close to the shore to go. The windward boats of course get the puffs first, but the wind is usually stronger a little farther out from shore, particularly if the shore is high. About all you can do is experiment and watch other boats. Heading up between puffs and bearing off with them will pay big dividends under these circumstances.

A run directly before the wind is likely to be the most heartbreaking part of a drifting match for the leaders as everything favors the boats behind. They very frequently pick up a puff and then when the puff dies, coast right up on the leaders on their momentum. This generally results in the boats being fairly closely bunched toward the end of at least the first downwind leg. When this happens there is a stunt which, if everything works right, will frequently let you catch a pack of boats that are a little ahead of you. This is to watch behind you and when you see a puff coming, reach past the sterns of several other boats until you have built up the maximum speed you can get, then head downwind again. If you timed everything right and if the puff was a little one, as they generally are in drifting matches, the speed which you built up by reaching before the wind got to them will carry you on past them by the time the puff dies. Save this stunt until fairly close to the mark when it will be too late for someone else to try it on you.

The main thing is not to worry if you are behind—you are probably better off than if you were leading—and do not start jumping around doing silly things just because nothing seems to be happening. Winning a drifting match is 95 percent luck—all you can do is to make the most of that other five percent.

The most important thing to *not* do if you are in the lead seems to be to try to cover the fleet by taking a middle course. There is no scientific reason that I can find for this, but on a number of occasions I have been well in the lead when the wind dropped. To play it safe, I thought, I would hold a middle course—and I have had boats sail around me on both sides. The only possible reason that I can think of for this is that when you are in the middle, you have a tendency to dash off in all directions and to be constantly trying to use someone else's worn-out wind instead of finding your own. There is a tendency, which is fatal, to watch other boats and try to get over near them just because they have a momentary puff. By the time you get near them that puff is gone, and before another one comes along there, there probably has been one back where you were.

If you happen to get a poor start and the first leg is a beat, it will not pay to tack purely for the sake of getting clear. The leaders can detect wind shifts much better than you can, and if you split tacks the chances are you are sailing off on a poorer tack than they are on. Also, it takes so long to get about with no wind and takes so long to get started again that each unnecessary tack is terribly costly. The best thing to do is just to tack with the leaders until the boats get spread out more, then go on your own if you think you can outsmart them. If they cover you, just relax and wait until later to get them.

In a drifting match be very cautious when on port tack, trying to cross in front of a starboard tacker. He may catch a little puff you don't get and catch you helpless. Also, if you decide to tack in front of or under another boat, be sure you have about four times as much room as you think you need. A puff of wind or a shift may alter your relative positions suddenly.

FIG. 64

This photograph, and those in Figures 65 and 66, are telephoto shots taken a few seconds apart at the first leeward mark in the 1949 Midwestern Snipe Championship. It is interesting and instructive to figure out who beat whom around and why.

FIG. 65

5988 was on the inside and ahead in Fig. 64, so had no difficulty rounding in second place. Number 9, although on the outside, was fairly well ahead and also had his wind clear, while those on the inside are pretty well blanketing each other.

FIG. 66

*6911 was on the inside and far
enough ahead so that 5985 couldn't
blanket effectively. Number 23 must
have gotten a good safe leeward
position on 4556 in order to be able
to sneak in ahead of 5985.*

8. Tides and River Currents

STRICTLY SPEAKING, THE TIDE IS THE PERIODIC RISE AND FALL OF WATER along the coast caused by the attraction of the sun and moon. The tide rises for about six hours, remains stationary for a short time, then begins to recede and falls for about six hours. The rise is the flood tide, and the fall is the ebb tide. The term "high water" is used at the peak of the flood tide, and "low water" is used at the lowest point of the ebb tide. The interval between two successive periods of high or low waters is approximately 12 hours and 26 minutes, which means that the time of high or low water is about 52 minutes later each day.

Twice a month, at the new and full moons, the attraction of the moon and sun is combined, and the highest tides will occur, which are called "spring" tides. Near the first and fourth quarters of the moon, the attraction of the moon and sun are at right angles to each other, and the tide is at its lowest. This is called the "neap" tide. The height of the tide varies greatly at different points along the coast. At the Bay of Fundy and similar points where the coast contains inlets which narrow toward their head, the tide is very high. A promontory such as the Florida peninsula tends to lower the tide. Also, tides do not occur at all places on the same meridian at the same time.

The rise and fall of the tide causes currents to flow into harbors, bays, sounds, and inlets when the tide is flooding and causes these currents to flow out when the tide ebbs. The amount of current depends on the amount of water that has to get through a given channel in the time available. Therefore, the velocity of the current flowing into a small harbor through a wide entrance will be much lower than that of a current flowing into a large harbor through a narrow entrance. A high velocity current can be felt for some distance from the inlet.

The term tide is generally used interchangeably between the true meaning of the rise and fall of the water level, and a meaning synonymous with current, and this meaning will be used in the following discussion. Also, no specific mention will be made of river currents, as they may be handled in exactly the same way as tides.

Local knowledge is of the greatest importance when sailing where there are strong tides. There are, however, certain general principles that apply everywhere and which will be discussed here. If you understand these general principles, it will be much easier to understand what the local experts are talking about in explaining the local peculiarities of the tide.

Tide is always strongest in deep water (in the center of a channel) and is generally weakest in shallow water (along the shore, or over a reef or bar). It will be slowed up, or may even be reversed, behind a point or a breakwater, but will be stronger at the end of the point. Its direction in the vicinity of the point will be affected for an appreciable distance out away from the point (Figure 67). The tide will be less immediately in front of and immediately behind an island, and will be faster between the island and the shore, if the island is large in relation to the total width of the channel (Figure 68).

The Hydrographic Office of the Department of Commerce publishes Tidal Current Charts which are very useful in providing local information. The charts show the relative tides at different spots, and show where the tides change first. They will also show where the tides don't behave according to the theories on how they should—which sometimes happens.

The most important thing to remember when sailing in the presence of tides is that the direction in which the boat is heading and the direction in which you are moving in relation to the bottom or anything tied to it may be far different. (See Figures 69 and 70 which conveniently ignore the effects of tide on apparent wind as that comes later.) The amount of the difference increases rapidly as the speed of the wind and the tide get closer together, and decreases as the wind becomes stronger in relation to the tide. Your course and speed relative to another boat are not affected by tide unless of course one has a stronger tide than the other.

What all this adds up to, as far as racing tactics is concerned, is that you want to be sure that the course you are heading on is going to end you up where you want to go after taking the tide into account and that in planning your course, you have planned it so that the tide will hinder you as little as possible when it is going against you, and help as much as possible when it is going with you. If the wind is strong and the tide weak, you can pretty much ignore it. If the wind is light and the tide strong, the tide is of

Effect of Bays, Harbors, Reefs,
and Points on Tide
(Ebb Tide)

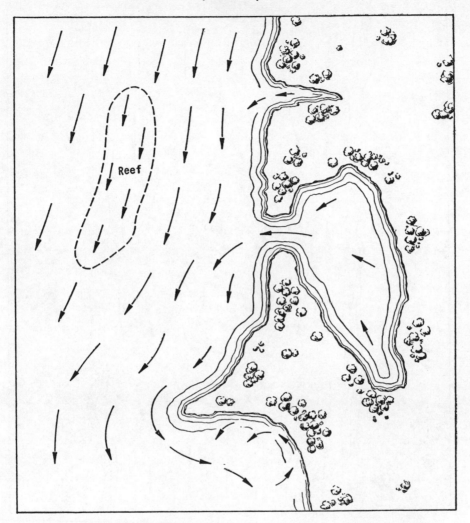

Reef

The length of the arrows is proportional to the velocity of the
current which is slowest over the reef and near the shore, and
fastest in the center of the channel, at the entrance to a large
harbor, and at the end of a point.

Fig. 67

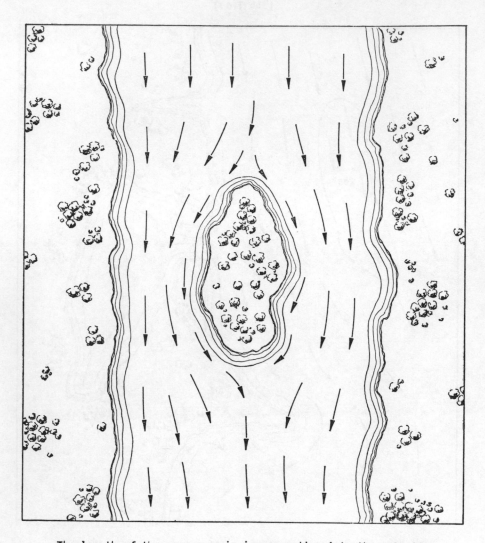

The length of the arrows again is proportional to the velocity
of the current. The current is faster between the island and
the shore than in the main channel because the water has less
space to get through, and is slower just upstream and down-
stream from the island.

Fig. 68

146

**Effect of Head Tide on Course Sailed
and Course Actually Made Good**

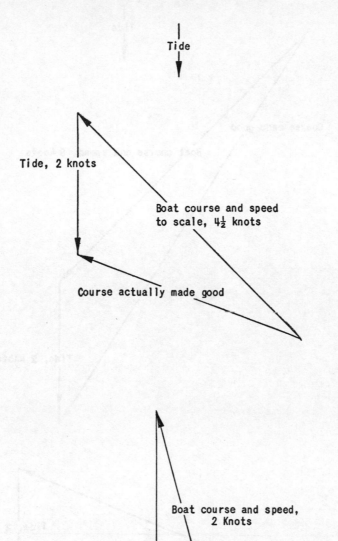

Tide

Tide, 2 knots

Boat course and speed
to scale, 4½ knots

Course actually made good

Boat course and speed,
2 Knots

Tide, 2 knots

Course actually made good

Fig. 69

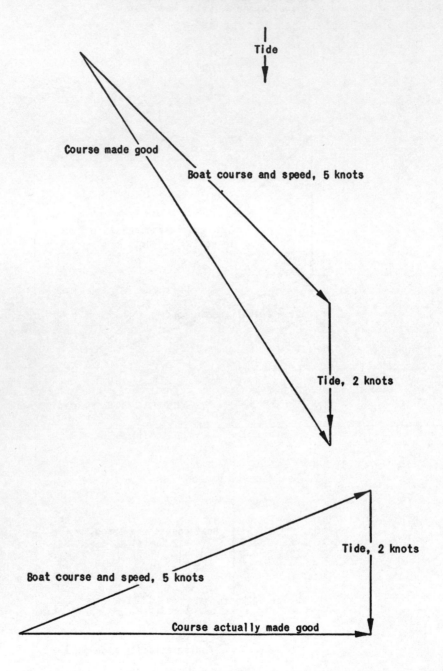

Boat Course and Speed
as Affected by Following or Beam Tide

Tide

Course made good

Boat course and speed, 5 knots

Tide, 2 knots

Tide, 2 knots

Boat course and speed, 5 knots

Course actually made good

Fig. 70

148

paramount importance. Between these two extremes, you must decide just how much importance to assign to the tide and how much more importance you should assign to watching your competitors.

Figure 71 illustrates the smartest trick—or most foolhardy, depending on how you look at it—that was pulled off at the Snipe World's Championship at Larchmont in 1949. In one of the races, the wind was about five miles an hour and there was a strong head tide. The Norwegian skipper had drawn one of those boats about which nothing good could be said, but the boat captain at Larchmont Yacht Club and all the men running the tenders there were Norwegian. All of the local skippers said to stay away from Hen and Chickens Reef as you would be sure to go aground, and the reef is hard. The Norwegians either knew better or they were awfully lucky—in any case, they only took two tacks on each windward leg—one to get them onto the reef, and the other which took them the full length of it—and took first place in a boat which in the other four races took two seventh places, one eighth, and one ninth. You can't ignore the tide when the wind is light and it is strong.

When beating against a strong head tide, be sure not to point too high. The importance of this increases rapidly as the wind decreases. Your speed over the bottom then becomes a small number which is the difference between two relatively much larger numbers—the speed of the tide and your speed through the water. Suppose the tide is running against you at two knots, and you are making two and a quarter knots through the water—leaving a quarter of a knot to get to the windward mark on. Now if you pinch a little and decrease your speed through the water by ten percent, you have cut your speed toward the windward mark by almost a hundred percent.

Another book on sailing recommends pinching when heading directly into a tide, on the theory that the tide will push against the side of the boat and squirt it to windward the way you can go way off to one side when you are riding on water skiis behind a motor boat just by aiming your skiis that way. If your sailboat were being towed by an infinitely long tow line at a steady speed this would be just fine—but when you have only sails and a wind, the theory is completely cockeyed. The tide does not affect the motion of the boat in any mysterious fashion—but it does affect the progress of the boat through the water in one way, and over the bottom in two ways. The first way in which it affects the progress of the boat over the bottom is by merely taking the boat along for the ride in the direction and at the speed at which the tide is moving as illustrated in Figure 67. The second way in which it affects the progress of the boat over the bottom and also through

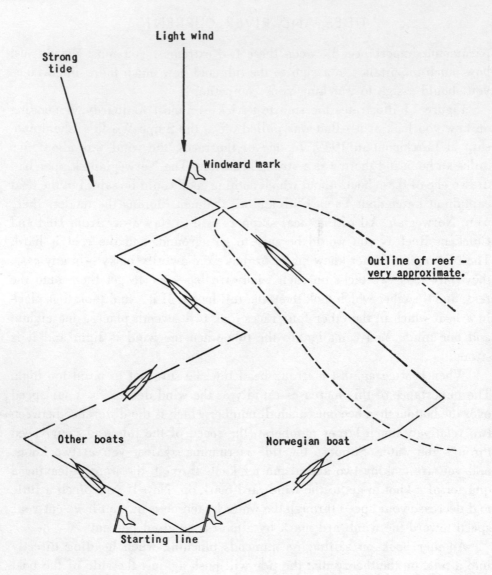

Light wind

Strong
tide

Windward mark

Outline of reef –
very approximate.

Other boats

Norwegian boat

Starting line

Whether they were smart or foolhardy or both may be argued,
but nevertheless the Norwegians ended up way ahead in the
third race of the 1949 Snipe Class World Championships at
Larchmont, in a boat that never placed higher than seventh
in the other races.

Fig. 71

150

the water, which becomes quite complicated if you try to calculate or illustrate its exact quantitative effect by vector diagrams is by altering the relationship between the true wind direction and velocity, and the apparent wind direction and velocity. This effect is a much exaggerated effect of the one illustrated in Figure 20, Page 49, which shows that a slower boat can head closer to the actual wind than a fast one.

It may be this effect that would cause a skipper who ought to know better to think he was gaining by pinching when heading directly into a head tide. What actually happens is that when heading directly into the tide, the velocity of the boat in relation to the true wind is greatly reduced, allowing the boat to head much closer to the true wind without actually pinching in relation to the apparent wind. The only thing that keeps the sails happy is having the apparent wind in the right direction—in beating against a tide in a light wind you can sail much closer to the true wind than without the tide and therefore get to windward better—but don't carry it to the point of pinching.

Figures 72 and 73 show the effect of tide on the apparent wind when beating to windward against and across the tide. The diagram illustrating beating to windward without any tide is not meant to represent the exact relationship of wind and boat speed for any specific boat, but it is representative of typical values for any small boat. The assumptions are that the most efficient course to windward is 45 degrees from the actual wind, and that a ten-knot actual wind will produce a boat speed of four knots. This results in the apparent wind making an angle of $32\frac{1}{2}$ degrees to the center line of the boat which remains constant as the most efficient angle for going to windward. In the examples of beating in the presence of tide, the diagrams were made by a trial-and-error method altering them until two requirements were met—the first, that the apparent wind must always make an angle of $32\frac{1}{2}$ degrees with the boat center line; and second, that the speed of the boat must be in proper relationship to the velocity of the apparent wind.

Figure 74 repeats two illustrations of Figures 72 and 73 showing a boat on both starboard and port tacks against and across a two-knot tide with a ten-knot actual wind with the wind at the best angle. It also shows a boat pinching one-half point closer to the apparent wind than in the upper illustrations. In this case the apparent wind and the true wind are from the same direction, and the course made good is directly into the apparent wind. The boat that is pinching is certainly going to windward—but it still won't get to the mark first.

When sailing into the wind or across it with a following tide, the effect

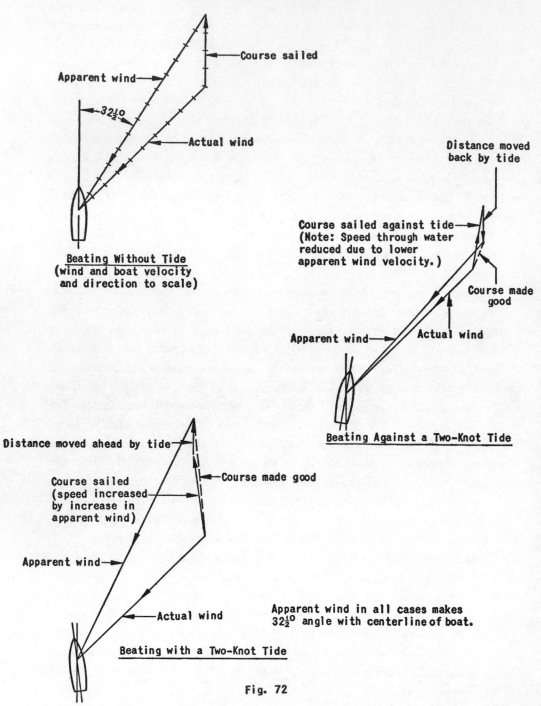

Beating Against and With Tides

Course sailed

Apparent wind

$32\frac{1}{2}°$

Actual wind

Beating Without Tide
(wind and boat velocity
and direction to scale)

Distance moved
back by tide

Course sailed against tide
(Note: Speed through water
reduced due to lower
apparent wind velocity.)

Course made
good

Apparent wind

Actual wind

Beating Against a Two-Knot Tide

Distance moved ahead by tide

Course made good

Course sailed
(speed increased
by increase in
apparent wind)

Apparent wind

Actual wind

Apparent wind in all cases makes
$32\frac{1}{2}°$ angle with centerline of boat.

Beating with a Two-Knot Tide

Fig. 72

152

Beating with a Beam Tide

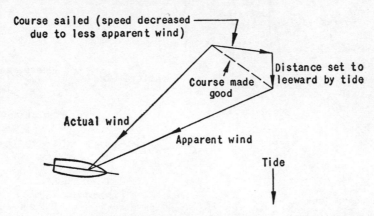

Course sailed (speed decreased due to less apparent wind)

Distance set to leeward by tide

Course made good

Actual wind

Apparent wind

Tide

Tide Setting Boat to Leeward

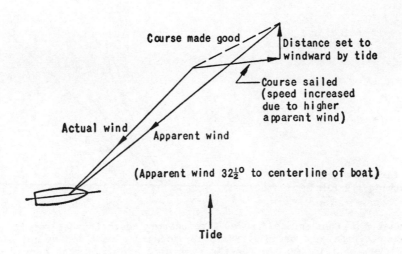

Course made good

Distance set to windward by tide

Course sailed (speed increased due to higher apparent wind)

Actual wind

Apparent wind

(Apparent wind $32\frac{1}{2}°$ to centerline of boat)

Tide

Tide Setting Boat to Windward

Fig. 73

153

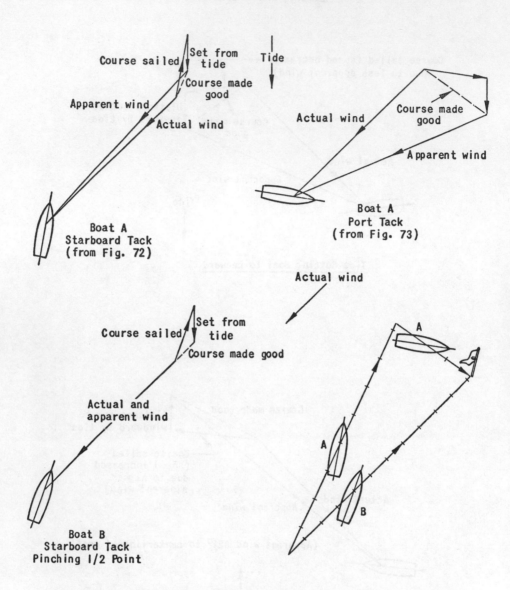

Boat B pinches one-half point when beating against tide, resulting in course made good being directly to windward. Boat A does not pinch. Since all diagrams are for the same wind and tide, the course made good for each diagram is to scale as to speed. To cover a representative distance to windward as shown, Boat B which pinches, takes 11.2 minutes, while Boat A, although traveling farther, takes 9.4 minutes.

Fig. 74

of the tide is to greatly increase the speed of the boat in relation to the true wind, thereby increasing the angle between the apparent wind and the actual wind and increasing the amount of the apparent wind. All of this is not actually as confusing as it sounds, as the skipper when racing is conscious only of the way his sails behave and of the direction of the apparent wind— he generally has no way of knowing the direction of the actual wind unless he is heading directly into it or out of it, and he really doesn't care.

When beating against a strong tide in a light wind, keep taking bearings on the shore to be sure that you are actually going somewhere in relation to the shore. When you find that you aren't—drop the anchor. If you can sneak it out without competitors seeing you, act as if you were sailing normally. They will see you suddenly start gaining on them and will start sailing frantically to go as fast as you seem to be going—and the harder they try, the faster they go backward.

Another good thing to remember when racing with a light wind and a strong tide is that the tide is obeying laws of nature and can be counted on to perform on schedule—and a light wind can't. If you are reaching in a light wind and the tide is pushing you to windward—stay well below the mark. If you get too far to windward, the wind may die and you may never get back to the mark against the tide. If you are well below the mark and the wind dies, the tide will help you get there. Conversely, if on a reach and the tide is carrying you to leeward and the wind seems at all undependable, stay well up to windward. If the wind dies, you can continue to reach for the mark, while the boats that headed directly for the mark in the first place will have a practically hopeless beat for it.

The effect of tides on starting tactics has been covered already, but might be summarized while we are talking about tides. With a head tide that is strong in relation to the wind, always hit the windward end of the line and stay very close to the line before the start. With a following tide and a light wind, hitting the leeward end is the safest; stay fairly far back of the line, and if the wind is very light, don't take any chances of being over early.

When sailing directly before the wind with a light wind and a strong following tide, tacking downwind is especially effective. The following tide has reduced the apparent wind—it may be practically nothing if the tide is strong and the wind light—and broad reaching off the wind will do a lot of good by increasing the apparent wind velocity and moving its direction so that it comes more from the beam and less from astern (Figure 75).

Local knowledge is particularly helpful when racing in a light wind at either high or slack water. The speed of the tide is of course zero at either

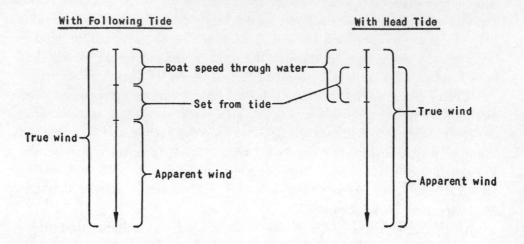

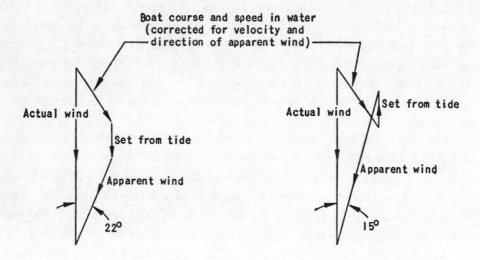

Heading out of wind by the same amount makes 50 percent more difference in direction of apparent wind with following tide as compared with head tide.

Fig. 75

high or slack water—but high and slack water don't always occur at the same time even over a fairly small general area. On Long Island Sound, for example, the tide starts flowing first along the shore. If you have a very light wind in which the tide will be very important, you may be able to get a boost in both directions, or at least a boost in one direction and no hindrance in the other. If it is close to slack water—and if the tide shifts first close to shore—you should stay close to the shore when heading in the direction of a flooding tide, and stay near the middle when heading in the direction of an ebb tide.

One of the things which often amazes people accustomed to making a scientific approach to the solution of problems is the frequency with which people arrive at the right answer for the wrong reason. It happens in any field connected with mechanics, science, physics and the laws of motion—and sailing is no exception.

Obviously any skipper who is successful in racing in the presence of tides knows all the tricks about sailing in tides—but it is amazing how many of them have the right answers with the wrong reasons. The main reason for this, I believe, is that very few people understand completely what tides do to the apparent wind. A complete understanding of this effect will explain the phenomena experienced sailing in the presence of tides, which are frequently ascribed to causes which just won't stand up under scientific scrutiny. Several diagrams of the effect of tide on apparent wind are given in Figures 72 and 73.

The term "lee-bowing" is used frequently in connection with sailing in the presence of tides. There seem to be several different definitions of the term, varying from the specific act of pinching when beating directly into a tide which has been mentioned earlier, to the general effect of the tide coming from the leeward side of the boat helping the boat to windward.

This effect is generally ascribed to the tide pushing against the centerboard or keel and squirting the boat to windward as if the boat were tied to something or were being towed. The statement is also frequently made that when the tide and wind are both more or less against the boat, the boat should head as close as possible into the tide when on a beat—which is correct. The reason given, however, is that this presents the minimum resistance to the oncoming tide, and that on the opposite tack the centerboard or keel presents a wide surface to the tide and as a result, which is of course most noticeable in a light wind and a strong tide, the boat will be set way off to leeward. The boat is set off to leeward on this tack, but not because of the width of the centerboard.

In solving any problem involving complex motions, the problem is simplified by considering the motions separately, then combining them. Let's assume that the tide and the wind are moving at the same speed and in the same direction. It is obvious under these conditions that *the boat is going to move with the tide, in relation to the bottom, in the direction of the tide and at the speed of the tide. It will go just as fast whether it is headed into, away from, or across the direction of the tide.* It can't do anything but just go along for the ride. It does not move in relation to the water, as there is nothing to make it move. A power boat with the engine shut off, a rowboat without oars, a Six Metre and a Moth under these circumstances will all move at the same speed, and in the same direction, in relation to the bottom, and none of them will move in relation to the water.

In the case of the power boat or the rowboat, if we start the engine or start rowing, the boat will then move in relation to the water. Its motion over the bottom can be plotted by drawing a vector representing the motion over the bottom due to the tide alone, in the proper direction with its length representing velocity, and another vector representing the motion through the water alone, in the proper direction and with a length representing the speed of motion through the water. The actual total motion over the bottom is the resultant of these two vectors, as shown in Figures 69 and 70.

This whole dissertation on the laws of motion should probably have been given earlier in the chapter, but it seemed that it might be better to give a general idea of the problems first, then to take up the specific problem of explaining the lee-bow effect, with a complete explanation. If this explanation seems too elemental, forgive me—but an awful lot of skippers with years of experience sailing in tides are going to disagree with me and I have to present an air-tight defense. A number of things said earlier will be repeated on the assumption that they may not have sunk in at the time, or may not have been accepted as facts.

As mentioned earlier—the problem of plotting the motion of a sailboat sailing in the presence of tides becomes quite complicated by the fact when the tide starts moving the boat around in relation to the bottom and in relation to the actual wind, the apparent wind moves around too. This effect would be hopelessly difficult to analyze when the boat is going to windward, except for one fact that we can safely lift from the science of aerodynamics. This is that for any given airfoil section (or suit of sails) there is one angle to the wind which will give the maximum ratio of lift to drag, and this angle is not affected by the speed of the wind within the limits of the velocities we are working with.

This fact justifies the assumption that for any given boat and suit of sails, the boat will go best to windward with the apparent wind at a constant angle to the center line of the boat. In Figure 72, this is shown to be $32\frac{1}{2}$ degrees for a typical small sailboat for which we assumed a representative speed in relation to wind velocity. We also know that wind velocity affects the speed of the boat, but this is a very complex ratio and no attempt is made to calculate it—a guess is good enough for the purposes of illustration.

In Figures 76 through 83, the effects of tide on apparent wind and on course made good are shown by diagrams for a complete racing course, with the direction of the tide in relation to the wind going all the way around the compass. The basic relationship of boat speed and wind velocity and direction is the same as in Figure 72.

The lee-bow effect is first apparent on the port-tack reach in Figure 77, where it is very slight. It is very apparent on the port beat in Figure 78, and also on the starboard reach in this figure.

On the beat in Figure 79 we have the case where one tack is almost directly into the tide. The correctness of the statement that most of your beating should be as near as possible into the tide is shown here as the starboard tack certainly doesn't get to windward very well—but it is the effect of the tide on the direction of the apparent wind combined with the tide setting the boat to leeward that is the cause, not the relative area of the centerboard. The same comments apply to the opposite tacks in Figure 82.

These diagrams also serve to illustrate what was meant earlier in this chapter when I said "you want to be sure that the course you are heading on is going to end you up where you want to go" and also that "the direction in which you are moving in relation to the bottom or anything tied to it may be far different." Don't forget what the lee-bow effect can do for you in taking you to windward—and also what a tide on your weather bow will do in the opposite direction when approaching a mark.

I mentioned earlier that pinching is very bad when beating directly into the tide. Pinching over a long period of time is never a good idea, but a tide on the beam setting the boat to windward lessens the effect of pinching, and there will be occasions when a little judicious pinching will be good tactics. In Figures 82 and 83, if you should find that you just can't quite lay the mark on the starboard tack, a little pinching will be better than coming about twice to lay the mark, particularly if there are boats behind you and to windward of you that you might not clear if you tacked. In Figure 78, if the windward mark were to be left to starboard, the same comment would

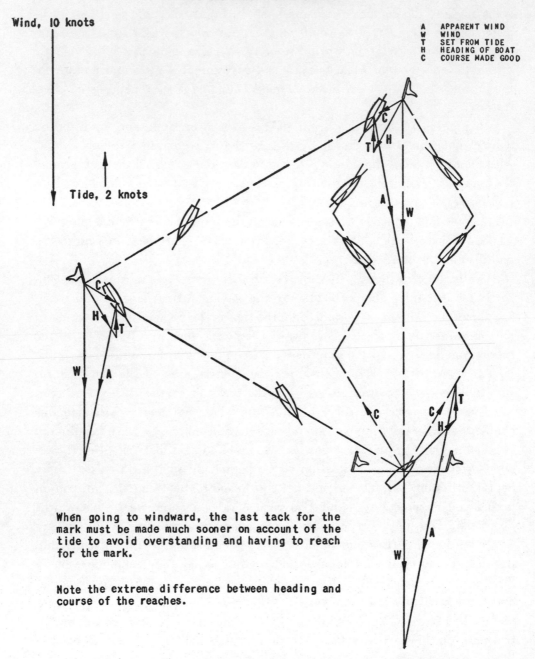

Racing with the Tide from the South
and the Wind from the North

Wind, 10 knots

A   APPARENT WIND
W   WIND
T   SET FROM TIDE
H   HEADING OF BOAT
C   COURSE MADE GOOD

Tide, 2 knots

When going to windward, the last tack for the
mark must be made much sooner on account of the
tide to avoid overstanding and having to reach
for the mark.

Note the extreme difference between heading and
course of the reaches.

Fig. 76

160

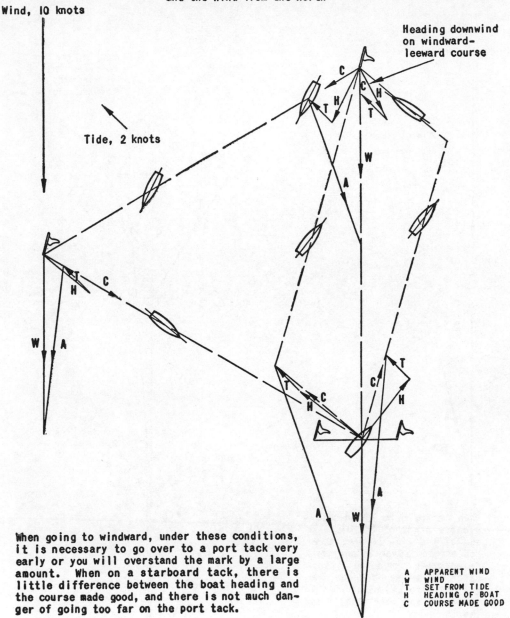

Racing with the Tide from the Southeast and the Wind from the North

Wind, 10 knots

Tide, 2 knots

Heading downwind on windward-leeward course

When going to windward, under these conditions, it is necessary to go over to a port tack very early or you will overstand the mark by a large amount. When on a starboard tack, there is little difference between the boat heading and the course made good, and there is not much danger of going too far on the port tack.

A   APPARENT WIND
W   WIND
T   SET FROM TIDE
H   HEADING OF BOAT
C   COURSE MADE GOOD

Fig. 77

161

Racing with the tide from the East
and the wind from the North.

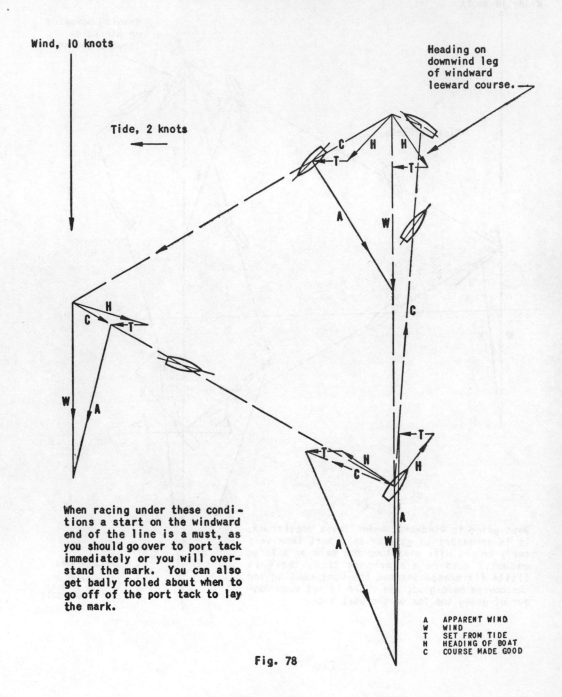

Wind, 10 knots

Tide, 2 knots

Heading on
downwind leg
of windward
leeward course.

When racing under these conditions a start on the windward
end of the line is a must, as
you should go over to port tack
immediately or you will overstand the mark. You can also
get badly fooled about when to
go off of the port tack to lay
the mark.

A	APPARENT WIND
W	WIND
T	SET FROM TIDE
H	HEADING OF BOAT
C	COURSE MADE GOOD

Fig. 78

162

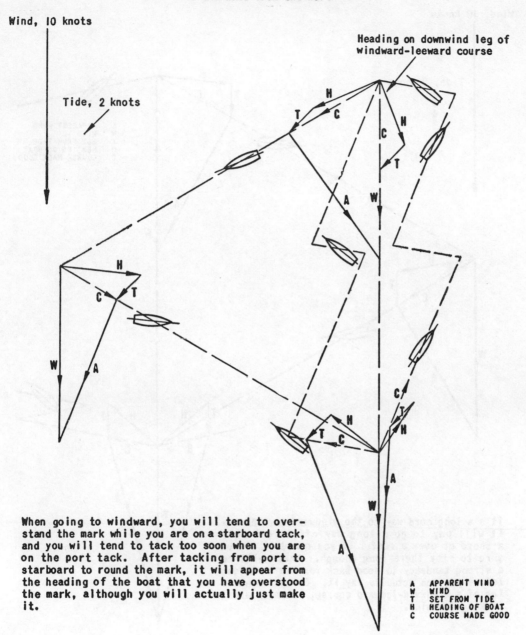

Racing with the Tide from the Northeast and the Wind from the North

Wind, 10 knots

Tide, 2 knots

Heading on downwind leg of windward-leeward course

When going to windward, you will tend to overstand the mark while you are on a starboard tack, and you will tend to tack too soon when you are on the port tack. After tacking from port to starboard to round the mark, it will appear from the heading of the boat that you have overstood the mark, although you will actually just make it.

A	APPARENT WIND
W	WIND
T	SET FROM TIDE
H	HEADING OF BOAT
C	COURSE MADE GOOD

Fig. 79

163

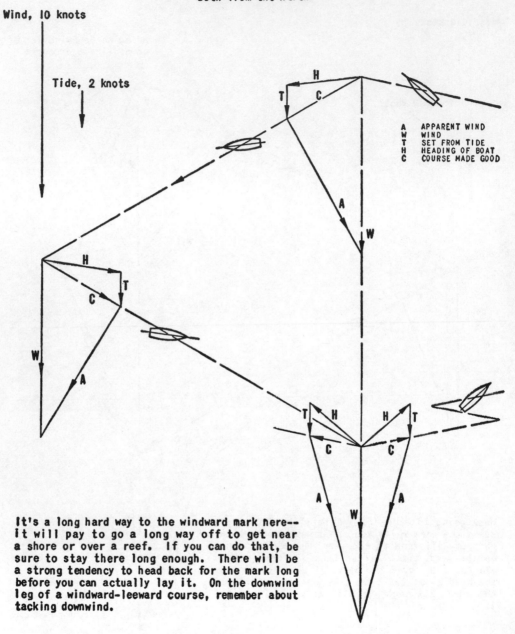

Racing with the Wind and Tid
Both from the North

Wind, 10 knots

Tide, 2 knots

A APPARENT WIND
W WIND
T SET FROM TIDE
H HEADING OF BOAT
C COURSE MADE GOOD

It's a long hard way to the windward mark here--
it will pay to go a long way off to get near
a shore or over a reef. If you can do that, be
sure to stay there long enough. There will be
a strong tendency to head back for the mark long
before you can actually lay it. On the downwind
leg of a windward-leeward course, remember about
tacking downwind.

Fig. 80

164

Racing with the Tide from the Northwest and the Wind from the North

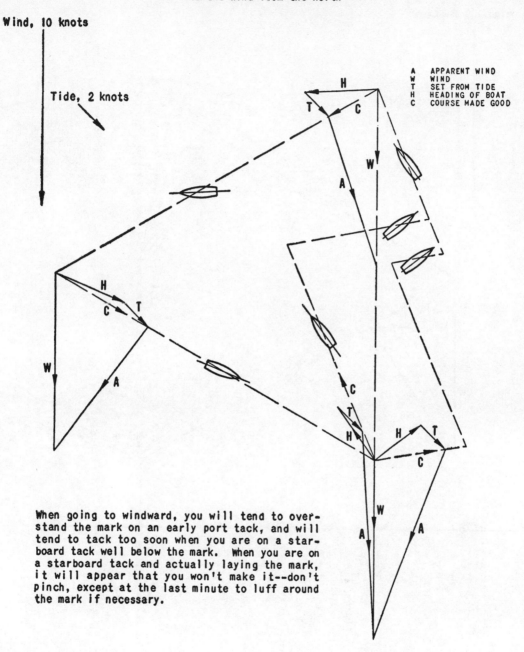

Wind, 10 knots

Tide, 2 knots

A   APPARENT WIND
W   WIND
T   SET FROM TIDE
H   HEADING OF BOAT
C   COURSE MADE GOOD

When going to windward, you will tend to overstand the mark on an early port tack, and will tend to tack too soon when you are on a starboard tack well below the mark. When you are on a starboard tack and actually laying the mark, it will appear that you won't make it--don't pinch, except at the last minute to luff around the mark if necessary.

Fig. 81

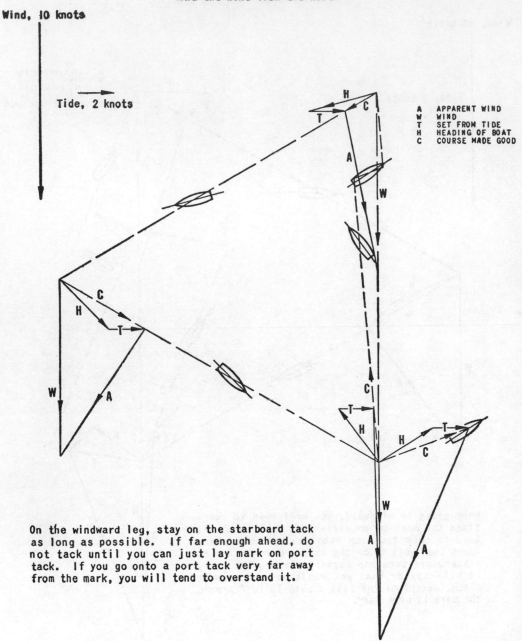

Racing with the Tide from the West and the Wind from the North

Wind, 10 knots

Tide, 2 knots

A — APPARENT WIND
W — WIND
T — SET FROM TIDE
H — HEADING OF BOAT
C — COURSE MADE GOOD

On the windward leg, stay on the starboard tack as long as possible. If far enough ahead, do not tack until you can just lay mark on port tack. If you go onto a port tack very far away from the mark, you will tend to overstand it.

Fig. 82

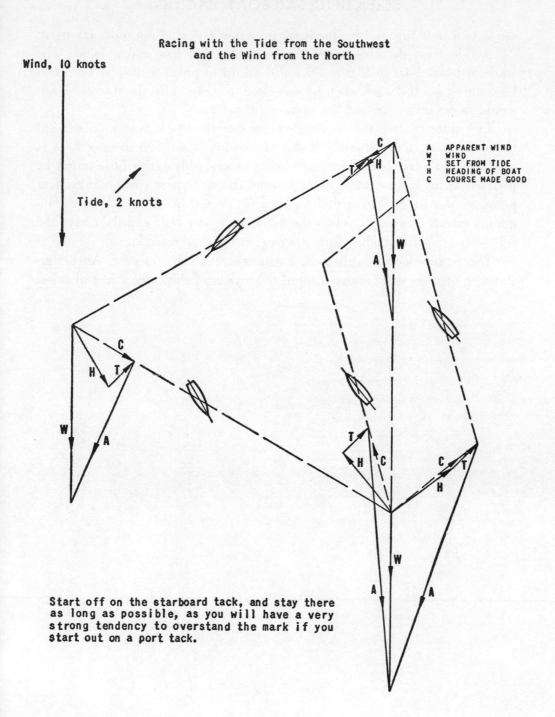

Racing with the Tide from the Southwest
and the Wind from the North

Wind, 10 knots

Tide, 2 knots

A   APPARENT WIND
W   WIND
T   SET FROM TIDE
H   HEADING OF BOAT
C   COURSE MADE GOOD

Start off on the starboard tack, and stay there
as long as possible, as you will have a very
strong tendency to overstand the mark if you
start out on a port tack.

Fig. 83

167

apply to a boat approaching the mark on a port tack and not quite laying it.

A tide from the aft quarter has a similar but less strong effect. The starboard tack boat in Figure 76 could afford to pinch a little if he found he couldn't lay the mark when he was close to it, and also the tide as shown would make luffing around the mark a lot safer.

In Figure 81, the tide is helping the starboard-tack boat to windward to some extent, but primarily it is just slowing it down. Pinching here is probably not advisable under any circumstances, although a little might be justified at the last minute. Luffing around the mark here can be quite dangerous—to a lesser degree than in Figures 79 and 80—but still to a dangerous extent, as you may clear the mark with your luff, and then have the tide set your stern onto it before you can get going on a reach.

The figures look complicated, but they are worth studying. An understanding of them will remove a lot of the mystery behind the effect of tides.

9. The Most Important Thing of All

AFTER YOU HAVE DONE EVERYTHING YOU CAN TO YOUR BOAT AND SAILS AND have studied racing tactics, there is only one thing left to do—get lots of practice. And that is actually the most important thing of all in winning races.

The more practice you have, the easier it will be to maintain your self-confidence, and the more confidence you have in your own ability the easier you will find it to win races. Many people on the coasts wonder how skippers sailing on lakes that are not even big enough for a good yacht anchorage can frequently do much better in big regattas than they should. The answer is simple—practice. With short courses and numerous laps, there is lots of practice rounding marks. And where you have to tack every few minutes or run out of lake, you get lots of practice coming about. The boats are bound to be closely grouped—they haven't any place to go—so you get lots of practice on rules and competitive tactics. Also, the skippers are delighted to get a chance to race on somebody else's mud puddle, so they frequently pack their boats on trailers and make round trips of 500 to 1000 miles over a week-end for a regatta. Practice under varying conditions. There is no substitute. Another excellent idea for a new skipper is to crew for an experienced skipper any time he gets an opportunity. He can learn a lot this way.

Race as often as possible in the stiffest competition you can get. When not racing practice starts, tacking, jibing, rounding marks, putting the whisker pole out and taking it in until you and your crew work perfectly as a team.

Keep notes on your experiences in each race for future reviewing. Write down the wind-and-water conditions, sails used, and details on any particularly bright or dumb things that you or anyone else did. You will find that reviewing these notes will be very valuable to refresh your memory, particularly at the start of the season. It will not hurt you any to review this book frequently, too; you will be surprised how some recent experience will give new emphasis to something said here which you did not take in at the time.

PART IV

Some Random Reflections
from Experience

I. The Vagaries of Wind

No MATTER WHERE YOU SAIL THE WIND CONSTANTLY VARIES BOTH IN DIRECtion and velocity, the only consistency being that the lighter the wind is and the smaller the body of water over which it blows, the more it varies. There are two types of variations which must be understood before the racing skipper can hope to cope with them successfully. I don't know of any recognized scientific or technical terms for them—maybe there are some—but I will call them temporal variations and geographic variations.

Mr. Webster says temporal is "of, pertaining to, or limited by time; transitory or temporary"—which accurately describes the variations in both wind direction and velocity experienced on a small inland lake. Temporal variations exist on large bodies of water also, but generally not to the extent that they do on small ones. The lighter the average wind is the more transitory and temporary the variations are. *These temporal variations usually move across the surface of the water and generally (but not always) will eventually affect everyone in a fairly large area.*

The favorite tricks of temporal variations are to pick up all the boats in the middle of the fleet and carry them up past the leaders who are just sitting frantically smoking cigarettes, or to pick up all the boats on one tack approaching a mark, either with a shift or an increase in velocity, and take them around the mark while the erstwhile leaders on the opposite tack sit and watch the parade. The puff will get to them shortly but in the meantime their outlook on life is pretty bleak. A typical example of how screwy they can get occurs oftener than anywhere else at the Missouri Yacht Club regatta when, five minutes after starting on a beat, boats are on both tacks close-hauled, on both tacks reaching, and running with their whisker poles out on both sides, and all going in the same direction. The boys who suggest paddling back to the dock and shooting craps for the trophy have something.

Geographic variations are variations in direction and velocity *which stay put in a given location for a fairly long period of time, and do not travel across the water like the temporal ones do.* These variations are of two types—predictable ones and unpredictable ones. The predictable ones are caused by the typography of the land surrounding the water, and may occur on small or large bodies of water. The unpredictable ones generally are characteristic of large bodies of more or less open water, where there is no obvious reason to suspect any dirty work. If I knew what caused these unpredictable ones I wouldn't spend so much time being in the wrong place at the right time when racing on large bodies of water. The unpredictable ones occur rather infrequently on inland lakes and fairly frequently on large bodies of water. The predictable type exist more frequently on inland lakes simply because the lakes are smaller and you are always racing much closer to the shore line.

Unpredictable geographic wind variations can cause a lake sailor a lot of trouble when he is sailing on a large body of water, because he is likely to think that no such thing should exist when he is a long distance away from shore and the shore line has no hills or trees on it. He is accustomed to coping with geographic variations by approaching shore lines gingerly and watching carefully to see whether the boats inshore are doing better than the ones off shore and vice versa and staying away from windward shores, but he is likely to get a little absent-minded when he gets on a large body of water, with the result that frequently when he finds out that there is a geographic variation it is too late to do anything about it by the time that he realizes that it exists. Deep water sailors get caught now and then too.

In the fourth race at the Snipe National Championship on Barnegat Bay in 1951, there were a couple of geographic variations which were about as unpredictable and about as big as any I have ever seen. Shortly after getting a good start on the leeward end of a starting line which greatly favored this end of the line, I decided that I had been on a starboard tack long enough and I had better go on to a port tack to go over and stay generally between the fleet and the mark. By the time I had gone back on a starboard tack I was ahead of all of the boats that were taking a middle course, but the boats that had held the starboard tack and hadn't gone on a port tack at all were way ahead of me.

At the start of the second lap I was pretty well back in the fleet and all of the boats ahead of me except one rounded the leeward mark and started off on the starboard tack which had paid off so well on the first lap. I decided to take a short port tack merely to avoid following directly behind everyone ahead of me, and found much to my amazement, that when I went on to the starboard tack I was pointing at least ten degrees higher than the boats which had taken a starboard tack directly away from the mark. With only a few short hitches on the port tack I was able to lay the mark on the starboard tack, moving up to second place at the second windward mark. A few of the starboard tackers either got smart after awhile and came on over, or got there accidentally as I did, but a lot of them just kept following the track that had been so successful the first lap and dropped back hopelessly, the boats which had been in the lead going back to about the middle of the fleet.

On another occasion in the Midwinter Regatta at Clearwater, Florida, we were racing in the Gulf and all the smart skippers knew that because of the tide, the only thing to do was to hold the starboard tack along the shore until you could lay the windward mark, then go out to sea. Carlos Bosch of Cuba goofed on timing his start by an even thirty seconds, so he started with his wind clear but could see no future in following the starboard tack parade. After going about a third as far as he should have gone on the port tack, he caught a geographical variation that let him tack and lay the windward mark. Various other tail enders peeled off the starboard parade down the shore and followed him around the mark, with the erstwhile leaders wondering who these jerks were sailing around the windward mark as if they were in the race. They were too far away to tell who it was leading the race that they thought they were leading. It didn't work the second lap.

The answer seems to be that you can never afford to just look for temporal variations, and if there aren't any, just assume that you can sail along watching the scenery. If you do, the scenery is likely to suddenly consist of boats now ahead of you that you had written off long ago.

Also, when one of these geographic variations exists, you had better detect its existence early in the race and get over there and take advantage of it just as soon as you realize it is present instead of staying where you are and hoping that it will eventually get over to you. They just don't move across the water the way that temporal shifts do—you have to go to them.

2. When in Rome

THE OLD ADAGE WHICH RECOMMENDS COPYING THE ACTIONS OF THE LOCAL boys when you are away from home has its limitations when an attempt is made to apply it to sailing under widely varying conditions. There are two basic problems which must be separated in order to get the answer. One pertains to tactics as affected by tricky local conditions in which local skippers may have an advantage due to their intimate knowledge with these local conditions. The other involves the difference in technique between sailing on large bodies of water with big waves and on small bodies of water with no waves.

Local Tactics

The value of knowledge about local conditions is pretty generally overrated. Usually any smart skipper would figure out most of the things for himself, and usually the problem is that you get so much advice concerning local conditions that you don't know which to ignore and which to follow. I have actually run into only a few cases where it was necessary to plan tactics on the basis of local advice. One of these cases was in Long Beach, California, where both in 1950 and 1956, it was almost always necessary to go on a port tack immediately after the start, and stay there until you either ran into a sea wall and had to go on a starboard tack until you could get on a port tack again, or without a sea wall, just hold the port tack until you could tack for the mark. The only time you didn't have to do this was on the very rare occasions when the wind was very light and shifty, when you had to tack on the shifts. With a light but steady breeze, you had to get in the groove. A similar condition seemed to exist in Havana when sailing inside the harbor. I was never able to figure out any logical reason why these conditions should exist, but they did.

At Green Lake, Wisconsin, they have one course in which the windward mark is just off of a cove, and the port tack approach is under a very high bluff and close to it. Any fool could plainly see that the way to sail that course would be to stay out in the lake, and come into the mark on a starboard tack. Only it doesn't work that way. If the port tack is parallel to the shore, or nearly so, the stupid port tacker gets to the windward mark hundreds of feet ahead of his smarter competitor who does things the way he is supposed to.

Local Techniques

The problems pertaining to technique which face the inland lake skipper the first time he gets on a large body of water with big waves and the problems facing the skipper accustomed to sailing on large bodies of water when he first tries lake sailing are just about equally difficult to solve.

With large waves and fairly good wind the lake sailor will not be too badly off going to windward; however, when he starts on a reach or a run he will think he has his anchor dragging. If he runs into a heavy chop or large waves with a fairly light wind he won't even be able to go to windward. On the other hand, the average deep water sailor having to cope for the first time with some of the things that are just normal on Missouri Yacht Club's Lake Lotawana, or Wichita's Santa Fe Lake, will be a likely candidate for a strait jacket to wear on his way to the padded cell.

Trying to do as the Romans do isn't very helpful in either case as the skipper out of his accustomed surroundings can't see that anyone else is doing things any differently than the way he is doing them.

Practice is the only thing that will enable a skipper to master the widely different techniques required, but here are some pointers on where to focus your attention while trying to learn.

Sailing on Large Bodies of Water

The technique for making a boat go to windward in high waves or heavy chop is logical and sounds easy—it simply involves not pointing too high. Unfortunately, in practice the lake sailor will find that it doesn't work quite as easily as it sounds and it takes quite a lot of experience to be able to master the technique. It is particularly difficult when the waves or chop exist in a moderate wind.

When I went to Havana in 1950 I had sailed in four regattas at Clearwater, Florida; three at Corpus Christi, Texas; and one in Long Beach, California, and thought I knew the answers pretty well when it came to handling waves. However, in two of the races in Havana on the Gulf of

Mexico the wind was from about six to eight miles an hour and the waves about three times as high in relation to the wind velocity as I had ever seen anywhere else, and I simply couldn't make any progress to windward. While I have won the Clearwater, Florida, Midwinter Regatta six times, and the Western Hemisphere Championships of the Snipe Class there once, each time I get there after not sailing during the winter, I have an awful time when there is a heavy chop and a fairly light wind. Sometimes I manage to get back into the groove again before the regatta is over and sometimes not.

The secret of success seems to be that the amount that you should bear off is very very slight and you must keep your eyes glued on the luff of the jib to be sure that you are pointing exactly where you should be. A microscopic amount too high and your boat just jumps up and down. A microscopic amount too far off the wind and you just fall off without going any faster than you would be going if you were pointing properly. You and your crew should also sit farther back on the boat than in smooth water.

As far as the technique of accomplishing this is concerned there seem to be two schools of thought. One of them maintains that the sails should not be trimmed quite as tightly, which automatically requires the skipper to bear off a little bit to keep his sails full. The other school of thought is to trim the sails where they normally would be trimmed without regard to the chop or the waves and then just keep the sails a little more full than normal by bearing off slightly. When I try the first method, the only thing I seem to accomplish is to not point quite as high as the experts and at the same time not go any faster. I seem to have better luck with the second method, but I have a lot of trouble even doing this if I haven't sailed in waves or a heavy chop for a number of months.

When the wind gets up to around fifteen miles an hour or higher the lake sailor won't have quite as much trouble going to windward in waves unless they are very steep and close together, as the boat then has enough momentum so that the impact of the waves doesn't slow it down as easily; however, it is under these wind conditions when the lake sailor will have his greatest trouble going off the wind.

The first year that I went to Clearwater we sailed three races on the Gulf, all of them in winds around fifteen miles an hour. I went to windward all right but on the reaches and the runs the Florida boats went by me like the Twentieth Century passing a slow freight. Running down the inside channel behind the island after the race was over, (where there were no waves) I could catch all of the boats that had passed me during the race, but unfortunately they didn't give any trophies for getting back to the Yacht Club first.

I was thoroughly baffled by the whole situation as I was sure that I was handling the boat as I always had handled it and there was obviously nothing wrong with the boat or the sails, as I could catch everybody on the way home; therefore, it has to be something that I was or was not doing in the race. Ted Kemensky gave me the answer—which is to not fight the boat on a reach and a run. It also seems to pay to move back a bit from where you would sit in smooth water, sliding even farther back whenever the boat starts to surfboard on a wave.

When reaching or running in a heavy chop or fairly good-sized waves, the boat seems to want to head in practically any direction except toward the mark. The lake sailor constantly attempts to correct these tendencies with his tiller—which seems to do a wonderful job of slowing down the boat. The answer is to let the boat go dashing off wherever it wants to as long as it stays within thirty degrees or so of the average course that you want it to follow. This involves keeping the tiller absolutely motionless except when the boat goes too far off of its course or when it looks like an accidental jibe might be coming up. There are a lot of other things which must be considered, of course, but I believe that the most important thing for a lake sailor to learn is that he must practically bolt the tiller down to the deck so that it can't be moved or he will be moving it a great deal more than he should.

Some other interesting problems come up in connection with going directly down wind when the wind is blowing hard and there is either heavy chop or high waves. In considering this question, it is necessary to separate the conditions with the heavy chop from those with high waves, as the technique is entirely different. In considering what to do under these conditions, it is also necessary to decide when discretion becomes the better part of valor.

When running directly before the wind with a high wind and *small* waves, the boat will plane very fast, and with the board up may develop an uncontrollable rolling tendency. This happens frequently on protected water and is not only disconcerting, but if it goes far enough to get the end of the whisker pole in the water you have either a torn jib or a broken whisker pole—or both. You may also go for an unscheduled swim. When this situation starts to develop, caution your crew to be ready to drop the board whenever you say to. About one complete oscillation is generally enough to indicate whether trouble is coming. If it looks like things are developing rapidly, have the crew drop the board when the boat is straight up, rather than waiting until you are heeled way over one way or the other.

As the waves *start picking up* (before they get high enough to surfboard on), there will frequently occur a combination of wave spacing and height which seems to make the boat want to become a submarine and sometimes the boat practically will not plane at all. When this happens, the standard method of unburying the bow by rapidly wiggling the tiller does not always work even when the crew and skipper are sitting as far back on the boat as they can get. In this case, the only method of getting the bow back up is to slack off on the jib sheet and let the whisker pole go well forward until the bow comes up, then pull it back again. It might be added that no sane person would have the whisker pole out under these conditions. I have often wondered if it would not pay to head far enough into the wind so that the boat would really plane rather than holding a straight course for the mark. This, of course, would mean an extra jibe and would necessitate traveling quite a bit of extra distance, but I have a suspicion that it would pay off.

When the waves are high enough so that the boat is surfboarding on the top of the waves when going down wind, the centerboard should be carried about as high up as you can get it, even though this increases the rolling tendency of the boat. The reason for this is that when the wave on which you are surfboarding decides to break, it practically throws the boat forward and the boat has a very strong tendency to switch ends. If it starts to switch ends and the board is down, you are over before you can do anything about it. If the board is up, the boat will merely slide sideways long enough for you to get things under control.

Sailing on Small Lakes

As far as technique is concerned the deep sea sailor will probably not have much trouble on lakes as long as the wind blows about fifteen miles an hour or more. He will find that he can point a little bit higher than he is accustomed to, and he should sit a little bit farther forward in the boat on reaches and runs than he is accustomed to when reaching and running on large waves. He should tack much more frequently than on a large body of water. When the wind gets light his problems increase rapidly. The wind will vary considerably in velocity with the result that the sails must be constantly retrimmed if the sheets are cleated, or if they are not cleated the tension on the sheet must be in correct relationship to the wind velocity.

The actual position to which the sails should be trimmed when on a beat does not change with different wind velocities, but if the sails are trimmed properly for a seven or eight mile-an-hour wind, they will automatically be trimmed too flat when the wind drops to three or four miles an hour unless the position of the sheet is changed because there is not as much wind pressure stretching the sails themselves and the sheets. When the wind picks up again in another minute or two the sails will have to be trimmed in again because the higher pressure will cause more stretch in the sails and in the sheets.

On a reach in a light wind it will generally pay to bear off somewhat in the stronger puffs and head up somewhat in the periods when the wind has dropped. For small variations, you might just as well hold your course, but in any case the trim of the sails will probably not remain constant for over a few seconds at a time if you are going to get the maximum performance out of the boat. Keep your sheets as slack as you can and still hold the sails full. The amount that the sheets are slacked off or trimmed in will be much greater on a reach than on a beat because on a reach, the position of the sail is changed; on a beat the sails are kept in the same place, the tension on the sheets being changed only enough to keep the sails where they belong.

In very light winds the crew weight should be shifted farther forward. When going to windward the boat should be pointed as high as possible without the jib luffing, and in fact with some jibs, the boat should be sailed with a slight luff in the jib all the time. The difference between pointing too high and not high enough is very small and constant attention is required.

Luck always plays some part in the winning of sailing races, and in races on small inland lakes in light winds, luck can play a big part. The important thing is to recognize this fact and not worry about it if you seem to be having lots of luck and all of it bad. The chances are that the breaks will even out pretty well in the end if you just relax and sail as well as you can; just don't write off everything that happens to you as bad luck without being sure that lady luck wasn't helped a bit by dumbness or a lack of alertness on your part.

Another good time to relax is on the start when the wind is very light and shifty. A perfect start is not worth too much under these conditions, as those behind can watch the leaders and profit by their mistakes. I don't mean to recommend throwing away your stop watch under these conditions, but if you are a little late on the start, have your boat moving and your wind clear and you are just as well off or maybe better than if you are out in front trying to cover the whole fleet. Sounds crazy but it seems to work this way.

The big problem in lake sailing is deciding when to tack on a shift and when not to. When the wind is more than about five miles an hour, it is generally best to wait several seconds after a shift seems to have occurred to be sure that the shift has actually occurred, and then tack. After tacking, make an immediate check on the new course to be sure that the shift has stayed with you. When the wind velocity is in the range of five to fifteen miles an hour, very frequent tacking will be necessary to take full advantage of all the temporal shifts which will occur. The decision on when to tack and when not to will cause the deep-sea sailor lots of trouble.

When the wind is around three or four miles an hour and occasionally drops to practically nothing, it is very difficult to decide what to do. You know that your jib has collapsed, but you don't know whether it has collapsed because there simply isn't any wind and your boat is still going on momentum or because the wind shifted. With this kind of a wind you will generally have a cigarette going to serve as a wind indicator, and the smoke coming from your cigarette can serve to give you a slightly more educated guess as to whether the wind has actually shifted or whether it has merely died. When your jib starts to collapse, look at the cigarette smoke and bear off a little bit in the effort to get your jib to fill. If the jib does not fill, and if the cigarette smoke shows that the wind is still coming from directly ahead, this probably means that the wind has merely died, and you might as well hold your original direction until you either run out of momentum or the wind picks up.

This may involve sailing for a fair length of time with the jib completely collapsed. However, if you attempt to keep the jib filled by bearing off, and your trouble is actually that the wind has simply died, you will find yourself going around in a circle and assuming that the wind comes back from the direction from which it was originally blowing you have lost a lot of progress to windward. If you decide to tack under these circumstances you will have a hard time getting about, you will lose all your momentum in the process, and will probably just succeed in getting about by the time the wind comes back up and you will have to tack again.

The geographic variations in wind on an inland lake can generally be predicted fairly well. When the wind is blowing off the shore it is not a good idea to go too close to the shore. If the shore happens to be a high bank or have high trees, it will pay to stay a long way out from it. On a reach there will be a strong temptation to go close to the shore because the boats near the shore get the puffs of wind earlier and look momentarily like they are making better progress. The only thing to do is to make up your mind as to how far off shore you think you should be, and then stay there. If you start changing your mind frequently as to where you should be, you will generally find out that every place you go you have gotten there just after the wind left.

When the wind is parallel to a shore line, the situation gets tricky and unpredictable. Sometimes you don't dare go in toward shore, and sometimes you don't dare not to. All you can do is to experiment cautiously and watch other boats carefully. Any variation that is found can generally be considered a geographic variation and the condition will usually exist for some time.

Considerably higher winds can be handled on small inland lakes, and in many cases these winds will be very gusty. Just be a bit careful on luffing the puffs when going to windward.

3. Using a Compass in Racing

A GREAT MANY PEOPLE SEEM TO BE BAFFLED ON THE SUBJECT OF USING A compass in connection with small boat racing, part of them being baffled as to why one should be used and part as to how. A compass is obviously not essential on a small boat as people have been winning races without one for years—there are, however, some occasions on which a compass is very helpful.

An experienced skipper can reach down a starting line and harden up on the wind and guess pretty well which end of the line will be the best end to start on without using a compass. However, in the excitement that prevails immediately before a start, he is likely to get caught starting on the wrong end of the line if the wind has shifted appreciably since he tried the starting line. A compass may help to avoid this. With a compass the first thing you do is to get the compass reading when reaching down the starting line on a starboard tack. In the illustration (Figure 1) the compass reading in this case is 180 degrees. Then if the compass reading when close-hauled on a starboard tack is over 45 degrees more than the starting line reading (more than 225 degrees) the starboard end of the line will give the shortest course to the windward mark. If the starboard tack close-hauled is less than 45 degrees more than the starting line reading (in example less than 225 degrees) then the port end of the line will give the shortest course. Sometimes considerations other than the shortest course will govern in deciding which end of the line to pick as covered earlier in this book.

In a high wind it is a good idea to keep an eye on the starting markers to be sure that they aren't shifting around; however, assuming that they are not, it is only necessary to remember the compass heading of the starting line and compare this with your starboard tack heading as you maneuver before the start. If you do this, a pronounced shift in the wind will not catch you starting where you wouldn't have if you had known better.

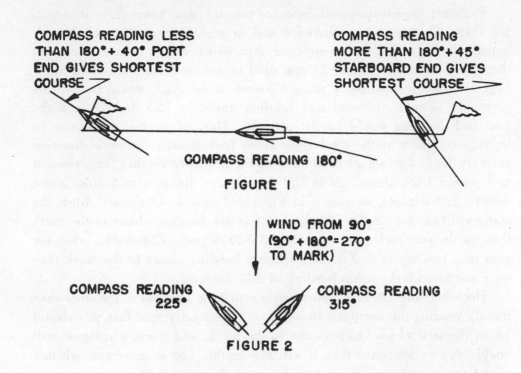

COMPASS READING LESS THAN 180°+40° PORT END GIVES SHORTEST COURSE

COMPASS READING MORE THAN 180°+45° STARBOARD END GIVES SHORTEST COURSE

COMPASS READING 180°

FIGURE 1

WIND FROM 90°
(90°+180°=270° TO MARK)

COMPASS READING 225°

COMPASS READING 315°

FIGURE 2

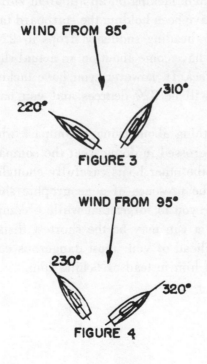

WIND FROM 85°

220°

310°

FIGURE 3

WIND FROM 95°

230°

320°

FIGURE 4

185

Probably the greatest usefulness for the compass, however, is in detecting shifts when going to windward and in making sure that you haven't gotten caught tacking on an apparent shift which wasn't an actual one. In the second example (Figure 2), the wind is coming from a direction of 90 degrees which means that a straight course to the mark would be 270 degrees, the normal starboard tack heading would be 225 degrees, and the port tack heading would be 315 degrees. This, of course, represents an average condition as the wind never blows from exactly the same direction for very long. The actual conditions would probably be that the starboard tack varied from about 220 to 230 degrees and the port tack from about 310 to 320 degrees, as shown in Figures 3 and 4. Obviously, when the starboard tack heading is 230 degrees you are heading closer to the mark than on the port tack with a heading of 320 degrees. Conversely, when the port tack heading is 310 degrees you are heading closer to the mark than on a starboard tack with a heading of 220 degrees.

Deciding when to tack and when not to tack involves a lot more than merely reading the compass. However, it is generally true that you should be on the tack which heads closest to the mark, and using a compass will enable you to determine this. It will also enable you to determine whether or not you have gotten caught tacking on an apparent shift.

If, for instance, you have been holding the starboard tack with a heading of 230 degrees, and your heading suddenly drops to 220 degrees, it will pay to come about. If you have come about on an actual shift, your port tack heading will be 310 degrees. If, however, you have tacked on an apparent shift your port heading will be 320 degrees and you had better get back where you were.

The most dangerous thing about using a compass while racing is that it is easy to become so engrossed in doing what the compass says to do that you may forget to watch the other boats carefully enough. This may cause you to completely miss the presence of a geographic shift when going to windward, and may cause you to forget that while a compass course to the next mark on a reach or a run may be the shortest distance to the mark, going off course to stay ahead of your most dangerous competitor may get you to the mark ahead of him instead of behind him.

4. Going to Windward

IN LOOKING OVER THE CORRESPONDENCE FOR ANY PERIOD, I HAVE NOTICED that a fair percentage of the letters that I receive are from skippers wanting to get to the windward mark sooner than they have been doing. The specific questions are sometimes, "How can I make my boat point higher?", "My boat points high in light wind but won't in a high wind (and vice-versa). What can I do about it?", "In our fleet, boats made by X point higher than boats made by Y, what can I do about it?", and from another part of the country, "In our fleet, boats made by Y point higher than boats made by X, what can I do about it?"

Almost everything that will be said here has been written earlier in this book, but maybe it will help to get it all pulled together in one place. In the first place—you have to start with the boat.

1. Is your mast far enough forward and your centerboard far enough back so that you have practically no weather helm? And is your rigging slack enough?
2. Are your jib fairleads properly located?
3. Do you have cleats for both the jib and mainsheets?
4. Are your centerboard and rudder sharp? Is the slot in the keel where the centerboard passes through it fitted closely to the board? And is the bottom smooth?
5. Do you have a mainsheet traveler which will permit you to strap down the main without pulling the boom in too far?
6. Do you have hiking straps for both the skipper and the crew? a tiller which is long enough to permit you to sit fairly well forward but not so long that it gets in your way when coming about? And do you have a tiller extension?
7. Is your boat fairly close to minimum weight?
8. Do you have good sails?

9. Does the stiffness of your mast suit your sails?

If the answer to any of the above is no, the remedy is fairly obvious. Getting to the windward mark first depends primarily on the skipper, but there is no point in handicapping yourself!

The location of the jib fairlead, for example, depends greatly on the jib that you are using. There are some makes of jibs which trim properly with the fairlead about eight inches in from the sheer regardless of wind velocity, while others should be on a track as close to the sheer as possible in light winds. In any case, it is necessary to provide fore-and-aft adjustment because in a high wind the mainsheet is strapped down tightly enough to pull the whole rig aft, which means that the fairlead should be about three inches farther forward in a high wind than it is in a light wind even with the same jib.

For those who still prefer to sail without cleats for the jib and mainsheets, I have no advice to offer except to look at the equipment on boats which consistently win races. For those who have cleats, the only thing to remember is that except in a very high wind when everything will be strapped down as tight as you can get it all the time, it will be frequently necessary to change very slightly the adjustments of the sheet due to the varying wind velocities—and by slightly, I mean adjustments as small as a quarter of an inch on the amount the sheet is trimmed in. On jam cleats for the jib, why not locate them so the crew can hang onto the jib sheet in high winds without the sheet popping out of the cleats?

On the subject of centerboards, the only conceivable advantage to a daggerboard is that the slot can be closed up tighter around the board. How much difference this makes, I am sure I don't know. In the last few years pivot board boats have won the United States and European Championships in the Snipe Class which would seem to prove that the effect is small.

The proper place to trim the main on any type of boat depends to some extent on the make of sails used, and this should be determined by experiment or by copying successful skippers in your class. The traveler used should be one which will permit strapping down the sails tightly enough so that the leech does not fall off without pulling the boom in any farther than it should be. There are some people who can win races with the knotted type of traveler, but there are more who can't.

Some people have gone a little overboard on the subject of tiller length. I have seen some, including a French boat which I borrowed at San Remo, Italy, on which the tiller was so long that the skipper had a tendency to get tangled up in it in coming about. If you want to sit that far forward, the best thing to do is to chop off the tiller until it doesn't interfere with you while coming about and then use a longer extension.

How much difference weight makes is very debatable, but I don't think that anyone will argue that a heavy boat has any advantage. If I had to choose between a good crew weighing 190 pounds and a fairly good one weighing 140 pounds, I would take the good one with the 50-pound weight disadvantage even in a light wind. I have also decided that the advantages to be gained from the use of a heavier centerboard have been considerably exaggerated. A lighter board is much easier to handle and gives an easy way to save some pounds. Also, with a well-finished boat I do not worry at all about the amount of weight that the boat picks up as a result of being left in the water; *however*, I also don't see any point in giving odds to anyone else by trying to race a boat that weighs more than a few pounds over the minimum.

On the subject of sails, I am becoming more and more convinced that knowing how to use a suit of sails and developing confidence in them is more important than small variations in the cut of the sails. Obviously, no one can win races with poor sails and it pays to buy the best sails that you can get; however, the leeches of all sails flutter a little bit, the jib will backwind the luff of the main on any full or medium sail, and in a very light wind, even a perfectly cut sail will probably develop a wrinkle along the front of the battens. If your sails are obviously no good, throw them away or keep them for moonlight sailing. If they have been made by a good sailmaker and have not been blown out of shape, stick with them and learn how to use them.

The argument about the superiority of a boat of make X versus one of make Y, within a one-design class, may be based only on imagination or may be based on the very real fact that some builder has tried to use all the tolerances in order to make a faster boat. I still maintain that in a one-design class, juggling tolerances will get you nowhere. The X versus Y argument in the Snipe Class has generally centered around two makes— one built to the exact middle of all tolerances, and one in which everything possible was done to create a new hull and still stay within the letter of the law. The argument isn't over yet but most of the heat has gone out of it. Judging from the correspondence I got on the subject when the argument was hottest, the relative merits were as follows:

1. On the East Coast, boat X was faster in high winds, especially on reaches and runs, but slower in light winds.
2. In the center of the country, boat X was faster in light winds, especi-

ally on a beat, and was slower in high winds.

3. On the West Coast, boat X was slower on reaches and runs in all winds, and faster to windward.

Could it be that the people sailing the boats had more to do with their winning than their hull lines?

So now, you have done everything to your boat that needs to be done, and have good sails: what next? The answer to that is easy on paper—practice and lots of it. If your sailing water has turned into a mud flat as Wichita's Santa Fe Lake has for the last five years, or if you live too far from your anchorage to sail evenings, this may be difficult, but practice is all important. And by practice, I don't mean just wandering around. If there is another boat that you can practice with (or against) so much the better, but you and your crew can do a lot by yourself. The standard complaint of the wife of a good racing skipper is "you never do any pleasure sailing—you're always pretending you're racing." Sad, but true—or it ought to be if you really want to win races.

It is pretty hard to tell when your boat is doing its best when there is no other boat around with which to compare your speed, but you can get lots of practice trying to keep it headed on a beat, just far enough off the wind to keep the jib full.

Whenever possible, try to practice with another boat with which you are evenly matched. Take turns sailing to windward, several boat lengths apart so neither is interfering with the wind of the other boat, but close enough so there will be no significant differences in wind velocity. One boat should experiment with changes in trim of the sails or changes in heading while the other tries to keep everything as constant as possible. This is a good place to find the perfect curvature for the foot of the jib, changing the trim of the sheet by $\frac{1}{8}$ or $\frac{1}{4}$ of an inch, and the perfect place to trim the main. It can be done while racing too, but it is hard to tell then whether you gained because you did something right or because the other skipper did something wrong. He may have been fiddling with things too. In any case—don't forget that when going to windward, your eyes belong on the luff of the jib—not on the scenery.

If there is a good breeze, practice luffing through the puffs, and don't stay on shore just because the wind is high. In most places—particularly at regattas—you will have to race at least part of the time in high winds, and it is on these occasions that lack of practice really shows up.

Coming about needs constant practice, as it is awfully easy to get sloppy on this maneuver. Except in practically no wind when you have to pump the boat around, and in a high wind and waves when you will find yourself in irons if you are not careful, you can just turn the tiller loose and the boat will get itself around somehow. If your mainsheet bridle is properly located, the boat will do a reasonably good job of it part of the time and a perfect job some of the time, but most of the time a little attention on the part of the skipper will result in a better job of coming about.

Have your crew watch the luff of the jib and turn loose of the sheet as soon as the luff shakes. This will be a little while after the skipper has moved the tiller, as the turning of the boat will keep the jib full for a short time. A good healthy jerk on the opposite sheet will start the jib over. In very light winds, it is possible to get the jib around quickly enough to be backwinded—which, of course, is bad—but otherwise it is only an exceptionally fast crew that can get the jib over too fast. The jib should still be fluttering when it is cleated down—if you can get it there that fast.

In general, come about on as large a radius as you can without slowing down too much. You can't help losing some speed in the process of coming about. Starting upward in the range of wind velocities from the pumping process necessary in drifting matches, the next step is to give the tiller a fairly good shove, let it stay at the limit of the travel for a moment, then ease it back to the center of the boat. A perfect job will be when you get the tiller back where it belongs at the instant that the jib fills.

The next step up, which means in winds of about eight to twelve miles an hour, the tiller should not go all the way over to the stop. Move it over fairly slowly, hold it there an instant or so, then bring it back to the center. Again—you will have done the job perfectly if your tiller is centered at the instant that the jib fills. With winds of from 12 to 15 miles an hour on up, you can start just letting the tiller go until it hits its stop (assuming that you have a mainsheet traveler that limits its travel to about what it should be) then pull it back. In very high winds, the whole performance will be accomplished as rapidly as possible—the speed at which it is accomplished gradually increasing from a leisurely pace at a wind velocity of 15 miles an hour up to not quite fast enough no matter how you try at a wind velocity of 35 miles an hour or over.

If you have a new crew, he will probably have trouble stepping or sitting on the sheet that he isn't pulling on while in the process of coming about. A temporary expedient until he has more experience is to have him throw the sheet overboard on the far side of the boat instead of merely dropping it when he starts to pull the jib over. After you have completed the tack, don't forget to retrieve the end of the sheet which is dragging in the water.

191

It won't slow you down much but it looks sloppy.

In high waves, try to wait for a moment when the waves are less high (waves generally come in groups and this usually happens), but in any case, don't crash into a wave while coming about if you can help it. Bear off a little just before you hit the wave, then as soon as the boat starts to move, slam the tiller over as hard as you can so that, if possible, you have things under control on the new tack before the next wave hits you.

Speaking of chop and waves, the technique given earlier will get the job done, if you have had enough practice to master it. The finest job of sailing in a heavy chop that I have ever seen was done by Clark King in the Snipe National Championship off of Alamitos Bay in Long Beach Harbor in 1956. The chop was made up of a very confused wave system coming from three directions at once, the wind was moderate, and the hot shots from all parts of the United States except California might as well have stayed home. (Unfortunately there were no Florida sailors there. They might have made life interesting for the natives.) There wasn't anything mysterious about what Clark did—he merely held the boat absolutely flat, bore off just the right amount at the right time, and kept his main trimmed perfectly all of the time. Immediately after the start, I was close enough to watch him, but not for long. I did everything he did but I didn't do it as well—nor did anyone else.

5. Just Plain High Winds

CONSIDERABLE SKEPTICISM IS SOMETIMES POLITELY EVIDENCED WHEN I write about sailing in winds of 35 miles an hour average velocity. The plain truth is that if you live in the center of the United States, and Wichita especially, you may not do any sailing before September if you wait for the wind to get under 25 miles an hour—which is considered just a nice invigorating breeze in these parts.

In the first place sailing in these winds is only practical where the water is sheltered enough so that the waves do not become dangerous, but those people who have inadequate bailing equipment and who stop sailing when their boats take on a lot of water won't get by here either, as you can take on lots of water in a high wind even with waves only two or three feet high. In England they build a small retractable self-bailing gadget which is fine for these conditions. It consists of two tubes, one inside the other, and when retracted, the bottom of the boat is smooth. When in action, the inner tube is pushed down about an inch and a half into the water. This tube is open on the back, and the suction created by the speed of the boat causes the water to flow out of the boat. They will not work if placed on the centerline of the boat immediately behind the centerboard, probably due to turbulent flow from the board. They should be installed at least two or three inches off of the centerline of the boat, on either side of the centerboard. Two are frequently used.

Racing under these conditions is just like any other racing—you have to have proper equipment and experience to be successful. Boats that are too lightly built or rigged will fall apart. Those without adequate spray boards, with too large cockpits, and nothing but a sponge to bail with will sink. And skippers who have always sat on shore when the wind blows will probably capsize. Some of the experts will now and then too, but not so often.

Put on the smallest, flattest mainsail you have—although this isn't so

193

important with synthetic sails. Drop your boom as far as you can, or reef if you can. Always keep the boat moving. Don't tack unless you have enough way to keep from going into irons. When tacking off of a reach, head up onto a beat and get things set before tacking. This is particularly important in tacking for the line at the start. If the wind is very gusty, use a little discretion in luffing into the puffs going to windward.

One of the fanciest maneuvers in small boat racing is jibing around the mark while planing at the end of the downwind leg. This maneuver requires perfect coordination of the skipper and the crew and the results are very easy to predict. You are either quick or you are wet.

Some people try to avoid this maneuver by going past the mark and coming about; however, those who have sailed in regattas in this part of the country in the spring have had plenty of opportunity to practice both methods of getting around the mark and quite a few more people have gotten into difficulty trying to go beyond the mark and come about than have in jibing the mark.

The best technique for executing a planing jibe is as follows: Get the centerboard down and the whisker pole in far enough ahead of the mark so there is no last minute frantic scramble. If the course has been a reach, head far enough above the mark so that as you make your final approach you will be dead before the wind. By doing this, it is usually possible for the skipper to get on the opposite side of the boat before the jibe takes place, and the jib can either be pulled over to what will be the leeward side after the jibe or simply left there (if you had your pole out), leaving then only the main to worry about during and immediately after the jibe. The boom jack should always be left on during the jibe and the crew should take hold of the boom, keeping an eye on the wind indicator and the mainsail and assisting the boom over when it is about ready to jibe.

The boom won't come over until it is ready to do so in spite of the efforts of the crew, but by the crew assisting the boom over, he can't be caught flat-footed by its coming over before he expects it to. The skipper trims in the main somewhat in anticipation of the jibe and tries to schedule the whole thing to take place just after passing the mark. After the jibe, the skipper lets the main run freely if necessary to hold the boat on the new course, then if the new course is a reach or a beat, starts trimming it in as rapidly as possible without making the boat heel too much. If the skipper and crew have had a great deal of practice together, the trimming of the main should be left to the crew as the skipper cannot handle the tiller and pull in very much mainsheet all at the same time.

When planing directly before the wind in relatively smooth water with the centerboard up, the boat will sometimes start an uncontrollable rolling for which there is only one remedy that I know of, which is to get the board down immediately. This rolling not only gives one a very insecure feeling, but if allowed to go far enough so that the whisker pole gets into the water, it can tear the lashing of your jib loose as it did to me once in Shreveport, or it can break your whisker pole and shoot the remaining parts through the jib, which happened to Harold Gilreath at about the same time. When this rolling starts, the smartest thing is not to wait and see whether it is going to be bad, but to assume it is and get the board down right away.

When going directly before the wind with certain wave conditions, the boat will tend to bury itself occasionally instead of planing as you would expect it to. Under these circumstances, with the jib out on the whisker pole or the spinnaker set, the last resort way to stop this submarining tendency is to let the pole go forward so the jib or spinnaker loses its drive. When these conditions exist secure the sheet to something so that if it is popped free from its normal trim position, it will let the sail go far enough forward to get the boat back under control, but not far enough so that you lose the pole.

6. How to Win Tune-up Races and Lose Regattas

THE LAST STAGE AT WHICH YOU WILL ARRIVE BEFORE WINNING REGATTAS consistently, and the first one at which you will arrive when you start losing your touch after winning some regattas, will be this nautical equivalent of being always a bridesmaid but never a bride.

The secret of success in winning tune-up races and losing regattas is to start doing stupid things under pressure. The best way to accomplish this is to not do enough racing. Reading or writing articles on how to win races or just pleasure sailing won't take the place of being in races. It has often been said that the best way to win a race is to get out in front at the start and steadily improve your position. Quite a few regattas are won this way because there is a definite advantage in being out in front; however, the racing competition in big regattas has gotten so stiff that even the skippers who are likely to win the regattas get bottled up occasionally on starts or take tacks which turn out to be sour and have to work their way up through the fleet; and the ones who win the most regattas are the ones who can't be counted on to stay bottled up when their situation looks hopeless.

One of the temptations hardest to resist is to immediately tack out and get clear after a mediocre start. Under these conditions, the wind in which you are sailing is badly scrambled up by boats ahead of you and the water is the same way. It is far better to just sit there and make the best of it for awhile until things settle down. If you can only resist that temptation long enough, it is amazing how many other people succumb to it and how much better off you are by just staying put (barring wind shifts, of course).

The next hardest temptation to resist is to keep going on a tack which has become sour because immediate tacking will put you behind some other boats. There is a terrific temptation to go just a little bit further so as to be clear before tacking. The trouble is that you generally have to go farther than you anticipate before you get clear, and all of the time that you are persisting on this tack, you are going in the wrong direction in relation to the people ahead of you that you hope to eventually overhaul.

The next thing that happens after succumbing to the above two temptations is to push the panic button. When you have done this, you start trimming your sails too tightly because everyone else seems to be pointing higher than you are; you start trying to go to windward by just aiming there; you start doing things quickly and jerkily instead of slowly and smoothly, and every tack you get on seems to be the wrong one so you come about again.

Which brings up the subject of the part that luck plays in winning races. If the wind shifts 60 degrees and the guy that you are on top of all of a sudden is on top of you, there isn't anything you can do about it. If the wind dies where you are and blows on everybody else, you can't help that, either. But you can be sure that you don't render any assistance to the bad luck in order to make it worse and that you take full advantage of the good luck.

Some of the races in a regatta in Shreveport a few years ago might be examined to see what light they can shed on this subject. In the second race, the wind was rather light and shifty and at the start of the second beat Bob Lawton was ahead, I was in second, and Harold Gilreath was several places back. I was keeping a wary eye on Harold, because I don't trust him even if he is several places back, and Bob was covering me.

About half way up the second beat, Harold was way off to port, and I decided that it would be a good idea to go over in that general direction. This direction didn't look good to Bob, so he kept on going. Harold and I either had a little better breeze or Bob got into a flat spot, because when we got back together again, I was in first, Bob in second, and Harold was in third. In this case, the flat spot that Bob got into was bad luck, but letting me get out from under him was poor judgment.

A little farther along, I was fairly well ahead of Bob but to leeward and more or less directly ahead of Harold when I sailed into a spot with no wind. Bob was still going like everything behind me and to windward, so I went about and he had to go behind me as I was on a starboard tack. So far, bad luck but no errors on my part; however, when Bob went behind me, he was still carrying quite a bit of momentum and I still wasn't going very fast as the wind had lightened a bit in general. Gilreath was still on a port tack and I decided to go back on a port tack, forgetting to keep an eye on what Mr. Lawton was doing in the meantime. All of a sudden he showed up on a starboard tack. I waited a little bit too long trying to decide whether I could clear him or not so that I had to bear off very sharply when I went behind him, with the net result that I was behind both boats (one error for Lawton, one error for Wells, none for Gilreath). The wind by now had become quite light and by the time we got to the windward mark, Harold was still in first place, but Chuck Hardy, who had gone way off to starboard, and Frank Riesenecker, who had gone way off to port, both came boiling up to the mark and I was in fifth place. I could still see the numbers on Harold's sails, but that was about all.

The next leg, which was the last one, varied between a run and a broad reach, and the first three boats behind Harold all started working up wind. There was no one close behind me, so the obvious thing for me to do was to head fairly far down wind, and hope (this maneuver only works if the wind is between a very broad reach and a run, if there is no one close behind you, and if everybody ahead is going to windward). What happened from here on out was a crying shame and could probably be scored either as a fielder's choice or as an error on Gilreath; but in any case, he elected to hold a straight course for the mark, not going upwind with the boys who went upwind, with the final result that all five boats finished within a second or two of each other with me in first place and Harold in fifth. I believe under the circumstances that this should be scored as an error for Harold, as I was far enough downwind from him that he couldn't slow me down by staying where he was; and if he had gone upwind with the other boats, he might have salvaged a second place instead of a fifth.

In the third race near the finish, Harold had a big lead in first place, Bob Lawton was all by himself in second place, and I was gaining rapidly on Eddie Williams and was about to pass him to pull into third place in the race, and first place in the regatta, because the wind had picked up and Eddie's crew was too light to hold the boat down. Then my crew, who was standing on the sheer because his tummy muscles had given out, proceeded to fall overboard trying to retrieve a jib sheet which had popped out of the jam cleat. This one, I am afraid, would have to be scored as bad luck for the crew falling overboard, but with a definite assist from me because I knew the jam cleats weren't holding very well and should have fixed them before the regatta or at least have sat on the sheet or tied it to something else so it couldn't go too far when it popped out.

Final result, Gilreath first place in the regatta, one error; Wells second place in the regatta, two errors.

MORAL: YOU CAN'T MAKE MISTAKES IN TIGHT COMPETITION AND WIN ANYTHING BUT TUNE-UP RACES!

7. Rejuvenating Old Boats— and Fleets

WHEN TRYING TO STIMULATE RENEWED ACTIVITY IN OLD RACING FLEETS which become inactive and in trying to promote greater activity on the part of existing fleets, one is frequently met with the objection that "our boats are old and heavy and we can't compete with these new modern light-weight boats."

No one can quarrel with the statement that the lighter a boat is, the faster it will go, all other things being equal; however, all other things never are equal and I think that the importance of minimum weight is considerably overrated. I have raced with crews whose weights have varied by as much as 45 pounds, and it is my opinion that being in the right place at the right time and not doing dumb things is so much more important that the 45 pounds difference in weight can be completely ignored.

A common complaint is that a heavier boat is no good in light winds. This statement is of course theoretically true. However, it is also true that in light winds being in the right place at the right time is of a great deal more importance than it is in higher winds. If a situation should ever develop where there was a light wind which never shifted in direction and never varied in velocity the lightest combination of boat, skipper, and crew would probably have an advantage—assuming that all sails were equal and all of the skippers were of equal ability which is an assumption which is not very valid.

A heavy centerboard is a definite advantage when a boat is just about to capsize; however, if the boat is sailed fairly close to vertical the centerboard is contributing very little to the stability of the boat. The boat is being kept upright by the skipper and crew getting out to balance it and by luffing when necessary. On any boat that is overweight I would use a board weighing as little as the rules allow in order to meet requirements.

In 1946 I was sailing Snipe No. 4225 and was quite successful in light winds, but I couldn't accomplish anything in high winds. This boat had a centerboard weighing about 58 pounds and I decided to buy a Varalyay with an 80-pound board to find out for sure if it was the boat or me that wasn't any good in high winds. There was no question about the ability of the Varalyay boat to go in high winds because I had seen them do it. After I got mine there was also no question about why 4225 wouldn't go in high winds. It was definitely the skipper and not the boat.

All of which I think adds up to the fact that there is no point in talking about two classes of racing boats under a basic class—one old and heavy and the other new and light; because the old and heavy one can be brought up to where it will compete with the new light one. The real problem comes from the fact that in any fleet where the boats have been allowed to become heavy and probably have poor finishes on them, the skippers are probably not particularly hot at racing or the fleet never would have gotten into that kind of condition. They therefore have two jobs on their hands, the first to rebuild their boats so the boats can compete and the second is for the skippers to get enough racing experience so that they can compete.

On a number of occasions I have sailed in regattas where the hot-shot from somewhere who had won all of the races for years in his own fleet but who had never sailed any place else was participating in his first regatta away from home. The result of course was inevitable—a few of them sneaked home and neither they nor their fleets have been heard of since. Most of them, however, took a good look at the boats, went home and started to work. They and their fleets have steadily improved ever since.

The moral of all this is that there is practically no boat for which there is no hope. There probably are some sails for which there is no hope. Not every skipper is willing to put in the time and effort to be a winner—but any of them can improve. Getting a new boat is the quick and easy way to improve on an old heavy one, but it isn't the answer to the question of how to start winning races.

8. Advice to Amateur Painters

SINCE PRACTICALLY NO SMALL BOAT SAILOR EVER STARTED PAINTING HIS boat as far before the deadline for finishing the job as he should have, the following advice is made available for racing skippers who have suddenly discovered that it is later than they thought.

In case you have bought a new automobile and your wife is tired of the color scheme of your old boat and thinks you should paint the boat to match the color of the new car, don't just go down to the dealer and pick up some of the automobile paint to do it. If your new car is one of the makes which is painted with enamel, this is fine; but if it is one of the makes which is painted with lacquer, you may get into a lot of trouble trying to put lacquer on top of enamel.

If the enamel is fairly new, chances are pretty good that the lacquer will simply lift the enamel in large areas of bubbles. If the enamel is old, the lacquer will probably start peeling off after a month or two. Du Pont and I presume many other paint companies make enamel to match all of the lacquer colors used by the automobile companies, and it is better to use the enamel and be safe instead of sorry.

There are, probably, still a few things that I haven't done wrong at one time or another in doing my own spray painting on a boat, but I don't think there are too many. I am convinced that the best thing to do is to take the boat to an automobile paint shop and let them do the job, yet I continue to do my own painting each season. Listed below are some of the better mousetraps to avoid if you insist on doing your own painting.

One of the most important things is to thin the enamel properly, using a fast drying thinner if you are spraying in cool or cold weather. Don't try to make any improvement on the percentage of thinner recommended by the paint manufacturer. If it doesn't flow through the gun properly, don't just add more thinner hoping that will make it work. The chances are that either the vent hole in the suction cup is closed up or that one of the small internal passages is plugged up if the gun does not spray properly with the recommended amount of thinner. Even when the paint comes from a brand new can and has been thoroughly stirred, it should be strained through a regular paint strainer or a discarded nylon stocking, because there are bound to be small pieces of undissolved pigment which will stop up the gun.

If you try to spray with too much thinner, the enamel will go on beautifully but it won't cover very well and, in an effort to make it cover, you will get nice big sags.

The other extreme of not using enough thinner will produce even more disastrous results. When you have used too much thinner, at least the paint dries rapidly and you can sand out the sags and start over again; however, if you use too little thinner with the theory that you will use higher pressure and get more paint on faster and cover better, you will accomplish all of that, except the stuff won't dry before next summer sometime.

Even with the proper mixture, the amateur painter spray painting only occasionally has difficulty in deciding how close to hold the gun to the surface being sprayed. If the gun is held too close, particularly when the surface has quite a slope, the material will be very wet when it goes on with a tendency toward sagging. If the gun is held too far away, sags will be avoided but the final paint job will have a lot of orange peel in it and will require a lot of sanding to look good. (The best way to do this job is still to take it to an automobile paint shop.)

One thing on which everyone agrees is that no polishing should be done on new enamel in less than a month and preferably six weeks. Some people say that the enamel can be sanded sooner than that and others say no. If you get a perfect paint job—which you are more likely to get by letting an automobile body shop do the job with automobile refinish enamel—you may decide not to sand the final job at all. It is possible, but not easy, to get a paint job practically free of orange peel, and yet without sags and runs, which really needs no final sanding. It won't be quite as good as the finish on the finest grand pianos, but can be very acceptable.

If you have decided to use metallic pigmented enamel, it is a good idea to decide at the same time to let a professional spray it. Another thing that may convince you to let an automobile paint shop do your next job is having the female member of the family find overspray on some highly treasured stuff stored in the garage which looked like junk to you and therefore you didn't cover it.

9. Protests and Protest Committees

EVERY NOW AND THEN AFTER A REGATTA, THE REGATTA COMMITTEE WILL congratulate itself because it has had a regatta without protests. If there have been no fouls which should have been protested, this is a fine record; but, if there have been fouls which should have been protested and if people go home griping about fouls which were committed and not protested, it is certainly nothing to brag about.

There is no sport in which sportsmanship is on as high a level as it is in sailboat racing; but, in my opinion, it is actually poor sportsmanship to not protest a foul which should be protested, particularly if the person against whom the foul was committed goes around griping that so-and-so fouled him but he didn't protest because it didn't affect his position.

There are some inadvertent and unavoidable fouls which are not a result of taking a chance with the rules in the hope of gaining an advantage. These, I think, should not be protested; they also should not be griped about.

If, however, you think that you have been fouled by another boat and the foul is not one of the excusable types just mentioned, the only sportsman-like thing to do is to protest and get the thing settled.

Fouls generally result from stretching luck too far in order to gain some advantage or in order to not sacrifice a position. A person doing this takes a calculated risk; and if he doesn't make it, it is not fair to others who have been more cautious not to protest.

Fouls sometimes result from people just not knowing the rules—or knowing them wrong. A protest is the only way to convince this type of offender that he should stop doing what he has been doing.

It also happens rather frequently that the person who thinks he was fouled doesn't know the rules himself, and no foul was actually committed.

In this case, if the person who thinks he was fouled doesn't protest, but goes around griping that he was fouled, he is not giving the alleged offender his right to trial by jury (the protest committee in this case); he is, in effect, trying his alleged offender in the headlines like some of our senatorial committees used to do.

It isn't necessary to mention that it is extremely poor sportsmanship to go around looking for opportunities to tag someone out, and I feel as though even if it is not required in the rules, it is good sportsmanship to hail another skipper when you have the right-of-way and it looks like you might get tangled up with him. 1 know I have been saved from trouble on several occasions and have been very grateful to a starboard tacker who showed up in a spot where I was sure no starboard tacker could be and who hailed me before I plowed into him on a port tack.

Small regattas should, and important regattas must, have a protest committee that knows what it is doing. The protest committee like the skippers should not go out of their way to cook up means of disqualifying people, but, on the other hand, they should not shirk their responsibility when a protest is filed and they should act promptly and firmly on any protest.

10. Helpful Hints to Regatta Committees

Since the prevailing weather at regattas is always lousy, the science of winning friends and influencing people among regatta contestants consists of making them want to come back again in spite of the things that couldn't be helped because of the excellence of things about which something could be done.

In an effort to compile a Dale Carnegie course for regatta committees, I have catalogued all of the important regattas in the past fifteen years which I have sailed in or watched listing their exceptionally good and exceptionally bad features, and came to the conclusion that with very few exceptions they could have been improved to some degree by giving a little more consideration to the fact which should be obvious but seems to frequently get lost in the shuffle—namely, that the visiting skippers like to have a good time, but primarily came to the regatta to race!

This lack of consideration usually arises from the fact that, while a few of the local skippers have attended equally important regattas, the majority of the members with whom they have to work have not, and their advice is generally ignored to varying degrees. Because these skippers who have been around still have to continue working and living with the other people involved, they are generally browbeaten into submission. However, since anything that appears in print automatically acquires a ring of authenticity, maybe in the future the suggestions contained here will help racing skippers who are working on regattas and are having a little trouble convincing other members of their clubs that things should be different on regatta day.

Race Courses

Most of the trouble with courses arises due to the fact that courses and starting lines which provide the best racing conditions frequently cause inconvenience for the racing committee and the spectators. In purely local races, since race committees are extremely hard to come by, life is generally made as easy for them as possible because their job is a thankless one at best. Also, the spectators on the club porch or float are generally families of skippers and crews or other club members, who, as cash customers, consider themselves entitled to a grand-stand seat where they can see the start and finish of the race.

These are perfectly valid considerations when laying out the starting lines and courses for local races, but they must be tossed in the ash can if you want to make friends and influence people among skippers who have come hundreds or thousands of miles in order to sail a series of races.

Permanently located markers almost invariably cause trouble. In the first place, some concessions have probably been made to the convenience of the spectators and the race committee in locating them. In the second place, the fact that the wind always blows from a certain direction insures only that the marks will be in the wrong place when you put on a regatta, because the wind always blows from a direction in which it has never blown before as soon as the regatta starts. Unless it is absolutely impossible because of depth of water, light buoys which can be shifted should be used. A very satisfactory buoy can be made from an automobile inner tube with a bushel basket inverted on top of the inner tube and painted with fluorescent paint and with a flag made of daylight fluorescent fabric about three feet above the bushel basket.

A fluttering flag is much easier to find than a cone on top of a pole, and the bushel basket, being considerably larger than any cone that can be put on top of a pole, also makes the mark stand out very well. The buoy should be weighted slightly to hold the pole perpendicular, and the mooring line should be weighted also so that it will run as nearly as possible vertically downward from the buoy.

At some places the water may be extremely deep, which makes it difficult, if not impossible, to use easily set marks of the conventional type. Havana, Cuba, is faced with this problem when sailing on the Gulf as the depth is so great that it is impossible to anchor a mark very far off shore except at one point off Morro Castle. When the wind cooperates, this allows them to sail a good windward-leeward course parallel to the shore; however, it is impossible to get a mark far enough out for a triangular course, and if the wind direction does not cooperate, they can't lay out any kind of a course using conventional marks.

They solve the problem by having a small motor boat serve as the off shore mark. By sighting on landmarks on shore, it is possible to keep the motor boat more or less where it is supposed to be and, in any case, the amount that the mark shifts position during the time that the boats are rounding it is of no consequence. When there is a strong current, it always appears that the mark has just decided to go home for lunch as you approach it, but you soon become resigned to the fact that this is an optical illusion and the guy in the boat really isn't playing games with you.

In any regatta, everyone agrees that all starts must be made to windward, but frequently not as much is done about it as might be. When a skipper has come a long way to sail in a regatta, he will not mind going downwind from the clubhouse a mile or so in order to get a full windward leg rather than to settle for a short beat to the first mark from a starting line more conveniently located. This generally involves beating the spectators out of a chance to see the start and involves a deviation from standard local practice, but it is a very important thing to do even in a relatively unimportant regatta if you want to convince the skippers that the contestants are more important than the spectators. On small lakes, it is frequently difficult to get any cooperation out of the wind and some rather weird courses may be necessary, but nobody objects to these providing maximum use is made of the available water in providing a beat after the start.

When the starting line is likely to be a long way from the anchorage, it is a good idea to announce this fact far enough ahead of time so that boats have no excuse for not being there on time and then the race should be started promptly at the advertised time. One of the regattas around this part of the country which used to be very popular has just about lost all of its customers because they never seem to be able to do anything on time. The last time I was there was several years ago, the wind was blowing between 30 and 35 miles an hour and the starting line was about a mile from the anchorage. I got out to the starting line along with several other boats about 15 minutes before the scheduled start and had an hour and twenty minutes practice at reaching and bailing before the race started.

There are, however, times when it is even more important to postpone a race than it is to have it on time. This is in case the wind has shifted so that what was intended to be a beat at the start has suddenly become a reach or a run or a one tack beat to the first mark. As soon as this happens, a postponement gun should be fired and, in these cases, it should be made clear that the postponement will not be for any fixed time interval and that the ten-minute gun will be fired as soon as the race committee has made another guess on where the wind is going to be and establishes a new course and a new starting line.

I have seen cases where one minute you would lay the mark on one tack and the next minute lay it on the opposite tack. In a case like this, if there is enough breeze so the race won't be a drifting match, about all that can be done is hit the average wind direction as well as possible and go ahead and hope; however, there is nothing more destructive to a visiting skipper's morale than having to start out on a leeward-leeward course or one in which no tacking is necessary on the alleged windward leg. He wants to get things started on time, but he would much rather sit around for awhile waiting for the course to be shifted than to start out on a course where there will be no windward leg or no tacking.

When sailing a triangular course, a reverse course signal is extremely handy, providing its use has been explained at the skippers' meeting. It is not nearly as confusing as it seems like it might be, and on several occasions I have seen it used to make a good race out of what would have otherwise degenerated into a follow-the-leader reaching contest.

The desired length of the course varies directly with the importance of the regatta, with the maximum length courses being desirable at the more important regattas where a large number of skippers have come a long way in order to sail. The courses should always be at least two laps in order to minimize the effect of tricky local conditions which may have trapped some of the skippers in the first lap.

Marks should be left to port whenever possible even though this, too, may cause some inconvenience in requiring the race committee to move some marks or to be otherwise contrary to local practice. Windward-leeward races should always be run with marks to port as there is never any excuse for leaving them to starboard, although I have seen it done.

In regattas where it is mandatory to have a certain number of windward-leeward races, these should be run off as early as possible. In a high wind, especially if there are likely to be high waves, a windward-leeward course is likely to cause a great many more casualties than a triangular course, and for that reason, windward-leeward races should be sailed where possible in moderate winds. The skippers who sailed in the Snipe Class United States National Championship at Corpus Christi in 1948 have long since found out that there is no point in talking about those races to anyone who wasn't there as all they will get will be incredulous looks. I'm not going to risk my reputation for veracity by talking about this regatta except to say that, if the third race had been windward-leeward instead of triangular, they would probably still be dredging Snipes out of the bottom of Corpus Christi Bay and that the reaches were the wildest rides that I have ever had. (That statement includes the days when I used to race airplanes, too.)

Starting Lines

Good starting lines are just as important as good courses, and they seem to be much harder to get. If a fixed starting line is normally used, such as one between a buoy and the end of the dock or a flag pole, any idea of using this in a regatta should be promptly forgotten. The chances are that at best some compromise is involved in either the direction or the location of the starting line, and, in any case, when the regatta comes, the wind is sure not to cooperate, so starts should always be planned to take place between a committee boat and a buoy and it is highly desirable to have another boat near the end of the line opposite to the committee boat to help in getting the numbers of early starters.

The larger the committee boat, the poorer the chances are of having a good starting line, because the larger the boat is, the harder it is to move when you want to move it or to keep from moving when you want it to stay put. Since it is almost inevitable that the line will have to be changed several times (especially if the committee boat tries to establish the line well ahead of time), an attempt should be made to browbeat the race committee into accepting the smallest possible committee boat with the biggest possible assortment of anchors and lines so that it can be moved easily and quickly in order to give a good line.

The all-time prize package as a committee boat was undoubtedly the 115-foot ketch (single screw, of course) used in the 1953 Snipe World's Championship at Monaco. All attempts to anchor it proved futile, and the starting line went leaping and bounding over about ten acres of the Mediterranean Sea. By pure luck, the starting lines were quite good when the guns went off and no Snipes were clobbered in the process, although there were plenty of near misses.

The only way I know of to tell whether or not a starting line is perfect is to have sailed around in the vicinity of the starting line long enough to know what the compass course is on the average starboard tack close-hauled, and then to take a compass bearing on the starting line. It is extremely difficult to establish a good starting line by merely watching a flag on the committee boat and sighting on the buoy on the other end of the line, and I don't know why so many race committees consider it a reflection on their ability to ask a contestant whether or not the line is all right.

When the wind is shifty (and when isn't it?), it is admittedly difficult to establish a starting line which will stay perfect up to the time of the actual start. The starting line can be moved, however, at any time up to the five-minute gun and frequently a little pulling in or letting out on the anchor line on the committee boat will accomplish wonders in keeping the sailors happy; and if the line really goes sour, no skipper is going to complain about a postponement signal any time prior to the start in order to improve the line. It is amazing the way some race committees turn a deaf ear to skippers screaming at them when the only similarity between what they have set out for a starting line and the correct one is that you have to stay behind both of them until the starting signal. The race committee doesn't lose any prestige by admitting that its line is sour—it loses prestige only by forcing the skippers to believe that it doesn't know what a starting line should be by its actions, or lack of them.

Where it is necessary to go a long way for a good windward start, no one will complain in a regional regatta about having an odd number of legs on the course and finishing at the clubhouse if the course has otherwise been good; however, in any regatta of national or international importance the course should be a standard triangular or windward-leeward one, and the race should finish where it started regardless of the inconvenience which this causes all concerned. The inconvenience of the skippers in this case can be greatly lessened by providing power boats to tow them home after the race.

A perfect starting line could probably be defined as one on which an experienced skipper without a compass would be unable to make up his mind as to which end of the line would be best. This can be accomplished very simply by giving the port tack end of the line about a five degree advantage; since the average small boat tacks on about a ninety degree angle, this means that the angle between the starting line and the starboard tack close-hauled should be about 40 degrees. If the angle between the starting line and the starboard tack is 45 degrees or more, there will be an increasingly large gangup at the windward end of the line as this angle increases; and since, in most cases, the wind is not steady enough to permit having an absolutely perfect starting line, it is better to err on the side of giving the port end more than it should have but only by a few degrees.

Since marks will be left to port if at all possible the committee boat will be (or at least should be—some race committees are a little casual on this) on the windward end of the line and a long anchor line will not interfere with the boats. If the wind is showing a consistent shift in one direction, an estimated amount of shift can be allowed for prior to the five-minute gun so that the line will be practically perfect at the starting gun.

The nervous tension is always high prior to the start of a race in an important regatta, and the racing skippers will remember the starting line long after they have forgotten everything else about the event.

There is no fixed rule as to the length of starting lines; however, a minimum is a little more than the total length of all the boats in the race. Lines much longer than this should be avoided simply because of the fact that the advantage occurring at one end or the other tends to be accentuated by a longer starting line.

The race committee boat is supposed to stay put after the start until it moves to establish the finish line. This staying in one place, however, is not too important providing the skippers know that during the race the boat will be moving around. It is, however, important that the committee boat should be on the proper end of the finish line and the finish line should be very carefully established so that it is absolutely at right angles to the course from the last mark. The line should be long enough to accommodate a fairly large number of boats trying to cross it at the same time. There is also no big mystery as to the proper end of the line for the committee boat on either the start or the finish. The rule is very simply that all buoys are left on the same side. If marks are to be left to port, the buoy should be left to port on the start and also the finish line.

Starting Procedure

Guns have a habit of going off when they shouldn't and not going off when they should, but everybody is accustomed to this and as long as the visual signals are correct only a minor amount of confusion will result from misbehaving guns. However, when the five minute signal is not exactly five minutes after the ten minute signal, the possibilities of confusion are terrific. It is impossible to guess whether the starting signal will be exactly five minutes from the erroneous five minute signal, whether it will be exactly ten minutes from the ten minute signal, or whether something new will be added and it will not be in proper relationship to either of these. When the five minute signal has been made at an incorrect time interval after the ten minute signal, the race committee generally knows about it and, if they don't, they will soon be informed of their error by frantic screams from the contestants. Unfortunately, many race committees exercise their prerogative of ignoring the contestants and letting them guess what's going to happen next.

Since getting a properly timed start is one of the measures of skill in sailboat racing, the only fair thing to do is to make a postponement signal and start over again. Some people may have missed the ten minute signal and have been counting on timing their start from the five minute signal, so that, even if the race committee gets honest and admits its five minute signal was haywire, they still may have eliminated the possibility of a number of boats getting a well-timed start through no fault of the contestant.

II. Psychology in Sailboat Racing

PSYCHOLOGY IS THE SCIENCE OF THE MIND, AND IT STUDIES THE BEHAVIOR of people. A discussion of psychology in sailboat racing involves a consideration of what effect the skipper's mental attitude may have on his racing performance. In my opinion, the effect is, in many cases, an extremely important one; and is a very appropriate subject to look at in the final chapter of *Scientific Sailboat Racing*.

You have all seen skippers who sail a perfect race now and then and a perfect series of races less often, but who never seem to end up on top at the end of the season. If these skippers could sail every race as well as they do some races they would be unbeatable. There is also another group of skippers who can make their boats go just as fast as anyone's boat when they are merely playing around or sailing in some race which has no importance, but who never manage to make the grade in tough competition.

Luck, of course, enters into these performances to some extent, but in the long run the breaks will be about even and it must be something else that causes this kind of result. This something else is the state of mind or mental attitude of the skipper.

The mental attitude of the skipper who wins consistently must always be one of complete confidence in the ability of his boat and his sails to win the race if he only handles them right; courage tempered with just the right amount of conservatism (an excess of either of these will get him into trouble); and a calm and cool appraisal of the constantly changing situations arising during a race. (I didn't really try to pick words all of which began with "c," but it turns out that way, and should make the lesson easier to remember.)

Confidence consists of constantly remembering that you have proven on numerous occasions that you can go just as fast as the other boats, on many occasions that you can go faster, and being convinced that you are going to win the race.

Courage consists of taking calculated risks when the odds look good enough, after applying just enough conservatism to be sure that you are being courageous and not just plain reckless, when it comes to picking a good spot on the starting line even though it is crowded; tacking for a safe leeward position instead of going behind another boat; cutting inside of a boat on a mark when it has rounded it sloppily, etc.

Coolness consists of keeping off the panic button when things don't go exactly the way you planned them, and remembering constantly that the race is not over until you cross the finish line and a regatta series is neither won nor lost until the last race is finished.

It's all very simple and logical and has all been proven to be true, but unfortunately the whole thing is a bit easier said than done. A knowledge of technique and tactics learned by experience plus constant effort to improve while sailing in as many races as possible in as tough competition as you can find is the solution to the problem.